KWELLER PREP

COMMON CORE

GRADE 3

ENGLISH LANGUAGE ARTS

Kweller Prep

Developed by a lawyer, Kweller Prep is an established supplemental education service with a 15-year track record of success in preparing students for specialized middle-school, high-school, college entrance, and graduate school exams. With thousands of acceptances to date, Kweller Prep has built a time-tested learning program with unsurpassed performance. Our competitive advantage is the way in which we operate; we focus on each child individually to ensure success.

Our rigorous program is designed for ambitious students to help them achieve their academic goals. Tutoring centers in Queens and Manhattan serve as learning incubators where parents, students, teachers, tutors, and counselors alike can learn from one another and grow. Nearly every tutor at Kweller Prep is the first one in his or her family to attend a Specialized High School or Top University on a scholarship.

Kweller Prep was created by the vision of Frances Kweller, attorney at law. She was the first one in her immediate family to attend both a top university (New York University - Steinhardt School of Education) and Graduate Program (Juris Doctorate - Hofstra University School of Law). In short, Kweller Prep is designed to help get you where you want to go! 2 locations! Forest Hills, Queens and midtown Manhattan.

Email : info@kwellerprep.com

Website: **www.KwellerPrep.com**

First Edition January 2019.

This is the first edition so if you find any errors, please correct the error and then take a picture of the correction and the page number. Please email it to info@kwellerprep.com. Ms. Kweller will you $1 for any typo you find before May 1, 2019.

TABLE OF CONTENTS

Introduction 4

How To Use This Book 5

Test Prep Tips 6

Reading: Literature 7

Ask & Answer Questions Using Text Evidence (RL.1.1) 8

Recount Stories & Determine Theme (RL.1.2) 13

Describe Characters & Explain Their Actions (RL.1.3) 17

Determine Word Meaning In Context (RL.2.4) 21

Identify & Understand Parts Of Texts (RL.2.5) 23

Identify Point Of View of Self & Author/Characters (RL.2.6) 26

Identify How Illustrations Convey Information (RL.3.7) 29

Compare & Contrast Narratives (RL.3.9) 32

Reading: Information 36

Ask & Answer Questions Using Text Evidence (RI.1.1) 37

Determine Main Idea & Explain Key Details (RI.1.2) 41

Describe & Understand Relationships Between Ideas (RI.1.3) 45

Determine Domain-Specific Word Meaning in Context (RI.2.4) 49

Use Text Features & Search Tools (RI.2.5) 53

Identify Point Of View of Self & Author (RI.2.6) 56

Use & Understand Information In Illustrations (RI.3.7) 60

Describe & Make Connections In Text (RI.3.8) 63

Compare And Contrast Key Points In Two Texts (RI.3.9) 67

Language 70

Demonstrate Command of Grammar & Usage (L.1.1) 71

Know Capitalization, Punctuation & Spelling (L.1.2) 73

Use Appropriate Language Conventions (L.2.3) 75

Determine Meaning of Unknown Word/s in Context (L.3.4) 78

Understand Word Relationships and Nuances in Meaning (L.3.5) 80

Know Academic/Domain-Specific Words (L.3.6) 82

Answer Key and Explanations 85

Practice Tests 97

Practice Test One 99

Practice Test Two 119

Practice Tests Answer Key & Explanations 143

INTRODUCTION

Common Core Standards

States all across the USA have implemented rigorous standards called the "Common Core Standards." These standards, or learning goals, outline what students in each grade should learn each year. They emphasize just how important the new goals are: they can help show whether students are on the right track to college and beyond, even when the students are years from those life stages.

State English Language Arts (ELA) Assessments

State ELA assessments are designed to determine whether students have mastered grade level appropriate reading, writing and language skills. The ELA assessments are usually given annually in grades 3-8, and are administered in either computer-based or paper-based format.

Question Format on State Assessments

All questions will be based on close reading of informational and literary texts, including paired texts. There are three major question formats on State ELA exams.

Multiple-Choice Questions: For multiple-choice questions, students select the correct response from four answer choices. These questions ask students to analyze different aspects of a given text, including central idea, style elements, character and plot development, and vocabulary. Reading and Language Standards will be assessed using multiple-choice questions.

Short-Response Questions: These are single questions which ask the student to make an inference (a claim, position, or conclusion) based on his or her analysis of the passage, and then provide two pieces of text-based evidence to support his or her answer. In responding to these questions, students are expected to write in complete sentences. Responses require no more than three complete sentences. Short-response questions will primarily assess reading, but will also require writing and command of language.

Extended-Response Questions: Extended-response questions are essay questions designed to measure a student's ability to write from sources, and prompt students to communicate a clear and coherent analysis of one or two texts.

HOW TO USE THIS BOOK

The objective of this book is to provide students, educators, and parents with practice materials focused on the core skills needed to help students succeed on ELA reading assessments.

A student will fare better on an assessment when s/he has practiced and mastered the skills measured by the test. A student also excels when s/he is familiar with the format and structure of the test. This book helps students do both. Students can review key material by standard through doing the skill-building exercises, as well as take practice tests to become accustomed to how the content is presented and to enhance test-taking skills. By test day, students will feel confident and be adequately prepared to do his or her best.

This Book Includes:

- 196 Skill building exercises organised by standard in order to help students learn and review concepts in the order that they will likely be presented in the classroom. These worksheets also help identify weaknesses, and highlight and strengthen the skills needed to excel on the actual exam. A variety of question formats are included in the worksheets to help students build skills in answering different question types, and to keep students engaged as they work through problems.

- Our ELA practice tests are based on official ELA reading assessments released by State test administrators. Our practice tests include similar question types and the same rigorous content found on the official assessments. By using these materials, students will become familiar with the types of items (including

Technology Enhanced Items (TEIs) presented in a paper based format) and response formats they may see on the test. Two practice tests are included at the end of the book.

- Answer keys with detailed explanations to help students not make the same mistakes again. These explanations help clear up common misconceptions and indicate how students might arrive at an answer to a question.

- The answer explanations for the practice tests also identify the standard/s that the question is assessing. If a student is having difficulty in one area, encourage the student to improve in that area by practicing the specific set of skills in the workbook.

- Test prep tips to help students approach the test strategically and with confidence.

TEST PREP TIPS

First of all, remind your student to pay attention in class throughout the year, asking questions as needed on homework and classwork. The Language Arts curriculum should follow the exact standards and skills that will be tested on the end-of-year assessment.

One of the best ways to prepare for a reading test is by—of course—reading. In the months leading up to the test, have your student read a certain amount of pages or minutes weekly from a book that she enjoys. Reading consistently will improve your student's reading comprehension and enhance her vocabulary, two skills that are crucial to success on the exam.

Another extremely effective strategy is to practice, practice, practice. Have your student work on practice questions and complete at several full length practice tests. Our practice tests are a great place to start.

However, simply answering the questions and then moving on will not yield much improvement. If your student misses a question, discuss why the correct answer is indeed correct. Come up with alternate approaches to this question type that may work better in the future. Have your student explain her answer to each question. This gives you the opportunity to reinforce logical thinking and correct misconceptions as needed. Plus, it's good practice for finding evidence to support a claim, perhaps the key skill on ELA reading assessments.

Prior to the test, encourage students to get a solid night of sleep and eat a nourishing breakfast.

For children, avoiding test anxiety is very important, so be sure to avoid over-emphasizing the test or inadvertently causing your student to feel excessive stress or pressure.

In addition, **teach your student general test-taking strategies such as the following:**

Narrow down your answer choices by using process of elimination. This involves crossing out obviously wrong answers to increase your chances of finding the correct answer.

If you get stuck on a question, skip it and come back to it after answering easier questions.

Remember that no one is expected to answer every single correction correctly. Don't panic when you get stuck on a question. Take a deep breath and remember that you are intelligent and prepared.

If you follow the tips here, your student should be well on her way to a stress-free and successful performance on this important assessment.

READING: LITERATURE

ASK & ANSWER QUESTIONS USING TEXT EVIDENCE

RL.1.1: Ask and answer questions to demonstrate understanding of a text, referring explicitly to the text as the basis for the answers.

Directions: Read the passage and answer the questions that follow.

Passage 1: The Cheeses That Ran Away
by Clifton Johnson

1   There was a man of Gotham who filled a sack with cheeses and started off for Nottingham market to sell them. He carried the sack on his back, and when he became tired he sat down by the wayside to rest. Thus he went on until he reached the summit of the last hill he had to climb before he came to Nottingham bridge.

2   There he rested, and when he rose to continue his journey a cheese slipped out of the sack and rolled down the hill toward the bridge.

3   "Ah! Mr. Cheese," said the man, "so you can run to market alone, can you? I wish I had known that before. It would have saved me the trouble of carrying you. Well, then, if you can go to market alone, so can the other cheeses, and I will send them along after you."

4   So he laid down his sack, took out the cheeses, and one by one rolled them down the hill. As the last one spun down the road he shouted, "I charge you all to meet me at the market-place."

5   Some of the cheeses went into one bush, and some went into another bush, but the man did not notice that, and he trudged on cheerfully to the market expecting the cheeses would meet him there. All day long he loitered about the market, and as evening approached he began to inquire among his friends and neighbors and other men if they had seen his cheeses come to the market.

6   "Who should bring them?" asked one of the market-men.

7   "Nobody," replied the man of Gotham. "They would bring themselves. They know the way well enough."

1. This question has two parts. First, answer Part A. Then, answer Part B.
Part A
Where does the man believe his cheeses are going?
  A. He thinks they're going into the bushes.
  B. He thinks they're running away.
  C. He thinks they're meeting him at the marketplace.
  D. He thinks they're going back home.

READING: LITERATURE

Part B

Which piece of evidence from the passage best supports your answer to Part A?

A. "Well, then, if you can go to market alone, so can the other cheeses, and I will send them along after you." (Paragraph 3)

B. "So he laid down the sack, took out his cheeses, and one by one rolled them down the hill." (Paragraph 4)

C. "There was a man of Gotham who filled a sack with cheeses and started off for Nottingham market to sell them." (Paragraph 1)

D. "Then he rested, and when he rose to continue his journey a cheese slipped out of the sack and rolled down the hill toward the bridge." (Paragraph 2)

2. What is one piece of evidence from the story that gives you a clue that the cheeses will likely not find their way to market?

A. "As the last one spun down the road he shouted, 'I charge you all to meet me at the market-place.'"

B. "Some of the cheeses went into one bush, and some went into another bush, but the man did not notice that..."

C. "Then he rested, and when he rose to continue his journey a cheese slipped out of the sack and rolled down the hill toward the bridge."

D. ""Ah! Mr. Cheese," said the man, "so you can run to market alone, can you? I wish I had known that before."

3. What detail from the text tells why the man rolled his cheeses down the hill after the first cheese escaped?

_____

_____

_____

4. What do you think will happen next in the story?

A. The cheeses will come to the marketplace and the man will sell them.

B. The man will never find his cheeses.

C. The man will find out that one of the other villagers took his cheeses.

D. The cheeses will come to the marketplace too late.

Passage 2: The Kettle That Would Not Walk
by Clifton Johnson

1   One day a Gotham man was getting ready to go to market, and his wife said to him, "Husband, we need a new iron kettle for the fireplace. Don't fail to buy one."

2   So the man bought a kettle at Nottingham, and toward evening he took it on his arm and started for home. But the kettle was heavy, and at length his arm grew tired with carrying it and he set it down. While he was resting he noticed that the kettle had three legs. "What a pity I did not see those legs before!" cried the man. "Here you have three legs and I have but two, and yet I have been carrying you. 'Twere fairer that you had carried me. Well, you shall take me the rest of the way, at least."

3   Then he seated himself in the kettle and said, "Now, go on; I am all ready;" but the kettle stood stock still on its three legs and would not move.

4   "Ah!" said the man, "you are stubborn, are you? You want me to keep on carrying you, I suppose; but I shall not. I will tell you the way and you can stay where you are until you get ready to follow me."

5   So he told the kettle where he lived and how to get there, and then off the man went. When he reached home his wife asked him where the kettle was.

6   "Oh, it will be along in good time," he replied.

7   "And what do you mean by that?" said she.

8   "Why," said he, "the kettle I bought has three legs, and was better able to walk here from Nottingham market than I who have but two legs. Yet I never noticed it had legs until I was nearly here. Then I told it to walk the rest of the way itself, for I would carry it no farther."

9   "Where did you leave it?" asked the wife.

10   "You need not be anxious," responded the man.

11   "I told it the way, and it will be along in good time, as I said before."

12   "And where did you leave it?" again asked the wife.

13   "At Gotham bridge," he replied.

14   She was not so sure about its coming as he was and she hurried off to get it, and when she brought it home the man said, "I am glad you have it safe, wife, for I have been thinking while you were gone that it might have taken a notion to walk back to Nottingham if we had left it alone there in the road much longer."

5. The man and his wife have different opinions about leaving the kettle to walk home on its own. Describe the man's opinion and the wife's opinion. Use details from the passage to support your answer.

Man's Opinon:

_____

_____

_____

Supporting Detail:

_____

_____

_____

Wife's Opinon:

_____

_____

_____

Supporting Detail:

_____

_____

_____

6. Which detail from the text explains why the man believes the kettle should carry him instead?

_____

_____

_____

_____

7. In what way are the cheeses from Passage 1 and the kettle from Passage 2 similar?
    A. They both refuse to walk.
    B. They both disobey their owners.
    C. They both run away.
    D. They both are sold in a marketplace in the end.

8. This question has two parts. First, answer Part A. Then, answer Part B.

Part A

What sentence describes the woman's feelings at the end of the passage?

A. She agrees with the man that the kettle will come home eventually.

B. She thinks the kettle will walk back to Nottingham.

C. She doesn't think the kettle will come home.

D. She thinks the man is lying and never really bought a kettle.

Part B

What happens as a result of the woman's feelings in Part A?

A. The woman gets mad at the man.

B. The woman goes to get the kettle and bring it home.

C. The woman tells the man to go get the kettle.

D. The woman and the man wait for the kettle to arrive.

RECOUNT STORIES & DETERMINE THEME

RL.1.2. Recount stories, including fables, folktales, and myths from diverse cultures; determine the central message, lesson, or moral and explain how it is conveyed through key details in the text.

Directions: Read the passage and answer the questions that follow.

Passage 1: The Ant and the Grasshopper
Adapted from the fable by Aesop

1   In a field one summer's day a Grasshopper was hopping about, chirping and singing to its heart's content. An Ant passed by, carrying an ear of corn he was taking to the nest.

2   "Why not come and chat with me," said the Grasshopper, "instead of working in that way?"

3   "I am helping to lay up food for the winter," said the Ant," and recommend you do the same."

4   "Why bother about winter?" said the Grasshopper. "We have got plenty of food at present." But the Ant went on its way and continued its work.

5   A few days later, the Grasshopper was playing a game with his friends when the Ant passed by, again bearing food.

6   "Take a break and come play with us," the Grasshopper urged the Ant.

7   "Winter is coming soon," the Ant told him. "I have to ensure my family has enough food."

8   "We have many days left until winter," said the Grasshopper. "All that work isn't necessary." But the Ant ignored the Grasshopper and continued its work.

9   When the winter came, the Grasshopper had no food and found itself dying of hunger. Every day, he saw the ants distributing the corn and grain they had collected in the summer.

1. Using the details from "The Ant and the Grasshopper," complete the sequence of events below.

(1) The Grasshopper asks the Ant to chat with him, but the Ant says he is putting away food for the winter.

(2) _____

(3) The Grasshopper again sees the Ant and asks him to come play with him, but the Ant says he has to make sure his family has enough food for winter.

(4) The Grasshopper says there is plenty of time left until winter and the Ant's work isn't necessary.

(5) _____

2. What is a main lesson in the fable "The Ant and the Grasshopper?"

_____

_____

_____

_____

3. Which detail helps to convey the fable's lesson?

A. "An Ant passed by, bearing along carrying an ear of corn he was taking to the nest."

B. "'Winter is coming soon,' the Ant told him."

C. "In a field one summer's day a Grasshopper was hopping about, chirping and singing to its heart's content."

D. "When the winter came, the Grasshopper had no food and found itself dying of hunger."

4. Why doesn't the Grasshopper want to work like the Ant? Use information from the passage to support your answer.

_____

_____

_____

_____

_____

_____

Passage 2: The Story of Icarus
Adapted from Greek mythology

1   A very long time ago on the island of Crete, a father and his son Icarus were imprisoned in a cave high above the sea. They had been imprisoned because the father was an extremely talented inventor, and the greedy King wanted the father to work only for him.

2   As Icarus became a teenager, he began to want a life of his own outside of the cave.

3   Icarus' father asked the King if he could let Icarus go, but the King refused his request.

4   When the father saw the disappointed face of his son Icarus, he knew that he must find a way for Icarus to escape. He gazed out of the cave and noticed seagulls flying high over the waves. At that moment, he had an idea.

5   For many days, the father and son collected seagull feathers. The father used metal frames to create two pairs of man-sized wings, and he attached the seagull feathers with candle wax.

6   On the day they planned to leave, the father reminded his son, "Icarus, remember not to fly too close to the sun. If you do, the wax will melt and you'll lose your feathers. Just follow my path." Icarus agreed.

7   As the father and son started to fly, Icarus loved the freedom he felt. He watched the seagulls soar higher and higher and decided to follow them.

8   "Icarus, stop!" yelled his father. "If you fly too high, the wax will melt. Not so high, Icarus!"

9   But Icarus didn't listen. As he flew even higher, he started to feel the wax melting down his arms. He saw his feathers slipping off and falling into the ocean. Icarus tried to fly lower, but it was too late.

10   The father watched in horror as his son fell into the water. He flew to shore to try to save his son, but he found nothing except a few seagull feathers floating in the ocean.

5. What is a lesson that readers can learn from the myth "The Story of Icarus?"

_____

_____

_____

_____

READING: LITERATURE

6. Which detail from the passage helps to convey the lesson in this myth?

    A. "As Icarus became a teenager, he began to want a life of his own outside of the cave."

    B. "As the father and son started to fly, Icarus loved the freedom he felt."

    C. "But Icarus didn't listen. As he flew even higher, he began to feel the wax melting down his arms."

    D. "For many days, the father and son collected seagull feathers."

7. Why are the father and Icarus imprisoned?

    A. They committed a crime.

    B. The King wanted Icarus' father to make inventions only for him.

    C. Icarus is dangerous.

    D. The King is evil and dislikes Icarus' father.

8. What would be another good title for this myth?

    A. The Greedy King

    B. Flying

    C. The Inventor and His Inventions

    D. The Disobedient Son

DESCRIBE CHARACTERS & EXPLAIN THEIR ACTIONS

RL.1.3 Describe characters in a story (e.g., their traits, motivations, or feelings) and explain how their actions contribute to the sequence of events.

Directions: Read the passage and answer the questions that follow.

Passage 1: The Camping Trip

1   All week long, Jessica and her friend Tia had been planning their first camping trip. It wasn't technically a real camping trip, since it would be in Tia's backyard, but they were determined to make it as close to camping in the woods as possible.

2   The girls planned to make smores, tell ghost stories, and look at the stars.

3   The day of the camp out finally arrived, and it was all Jessica and Tia could talk about at school. Later that night, the girls set up their sleeping bags in Tia's backyard. They made a pretend tent by throwing a sheet over some tree branches.

4   First, the girls decided to make smores. "You brought the marshmallows, right Jessica?" asked Tia.

5   "Oh no!" said Jessica. "I forgot the marshmallows!"

6   Tia didn't want to make Jessica feel bad, so she said, "That's okay. We can just eat chocolate and graham crackers!" It wasn't the same, but the girls pretended they were eating real smores.

7   Next, they decided to look at the stars. But the sky was dark and overcast, and there were no stars to be seen.

8   "Well, let's try telling ghost stories," said Tia. The girls started telling spooky stories, and they were having a great time. Then, suddenly, big drops of rain started pouring down.

9   The girls ran inside. Instead of feeling disappointed, they started planning an even better camping trip for another day.

1. Many problems happen on Tia and Jessica's camp out. What do Tia and Jessica's reactions to these problems tell you about them?
    A. They don't like camping very much.
    B. They both have positive attitudes.
    C. They will probably never try to camp again.
    D. They have a good sense of humor.

2. When Jessica forgets the marshmallows, Tia says, "That's okay. We can just eat chocolate and graham crackers!" What does this tell you about Tia as a character?

    A. She's a good friend.

    B. She doesn't like marshmallows.

    C. She's selfish.

    D. She's forgetful.

3. Would you like to be friends with Jessica and Tia? Use details from the story to support your answer.

4. Select two details that show Tia and Jessica are flexible when things don't go the way they planned.

    ☐ "The girls planned to make smores, tell ghost stories, and look at the stars." (Paragraph 2)

    ☐ "It wasn't the same, but the girls pretended they were eating real smores." (Paragraph 6)

    ☐ "The girls started telling spooky stories, and they were having a great time." (Paragraph 8)

    ☐ "Instead of feeling disappointed, they started planning an even better camping trip for another day." (Paragraph 9)

Passage 2: Leaf Games

1   Lauren pouted as she dragged the rake across the fallen leaves for what felt like the hundredth time. "I'm going to be out here all day," she sighed.

2   Just then, her neighbor Drew rode by on his red bicycle. "Hey!" said Drew. "You look like you could use some help."

3   Lauren was shocked. She couldn't imagine that anyone would ever volunteer to help with such a boring task. "Are you sure?" she asked.

4   Drew got off his bike and walked over to Lauren. "Of course!" he said. "Let's do a leaf jump." Drew ran and jumped into one of the piles Lauren had raked, scattering leaves everywhere.

5   "You try!" said Drew.

6   Lauren ran and jumped into another pile. "That is pretty fun!" she said, laughing. "But we're making a big mess."

7   Drew looked around. "True," he said. "Okay, let's do a race. You use this rake and I'll use this one. We have to race across the yard while dragging the rake behind us to rake these leaves. First one to the other side wins. Got it?"

8   "Got it!" said Lauren. She and Drew started running across the yard, dragging the rakes behind them. Drew got to the other side first, but Lauren challenged him to a rematch. "It was my first try!" she explained.

9   At dinner that night, Lauren's parents told her she had done a great job raking the leaves. "That might have to be your chore from now on," said Lauren's dad.

10 Lauren smiled. "Okay!" she said. "Raking leaves isn't so bad."

5. How does Lauren's attitude about raking leaves change from the beginning of the story to the end? Use details from the passage to support your answer.

_____

_____

_____

_____

_____

_____

6. This question has two parts. First, answer Part A. Then, answer Part B.

Part A

How is Drew in Passage 2 similar to Jessica and Tia in Passage 1?

    A. He can make the best of a bad situation.

    B. He likes the outdoors.

    C. He has a good sense of humor.

    D. He's good at playing games.

Part B

What detail from Passage 2 best supports your answer in Part A?

    A. "Just then, her neighbor Drew rode by on his red bicycle." (Paragraph 2)

    B. "Drew got off his bike and walked over to Lauren." (Paragraph 4)

    C. "'Of course!' he said. 'Let's do a leaf jump!'" (Paragraph 4)

    D. "'You try!' said Drew." (Paragraph 5)

7. Do you think that Drew is a good friend? Use details from the passage to support your response.

8. How do Lauren and Drew's feelings about raking leaves at the beginning of the passage differ? Use details from the passage to support your answer.

Lauren:

Supporting Detail:

Drew:

Supporting Detail:

READING: LITERATURE

DETERMINE WORD MEANING IN CONTEXT

RL.2.4 Determine the meaning of words and phrases as they are used in a text, distinguishing literal from nonliteral language.

Directions: Answer the questions below.

It was the day of the school spelling bee, and I was sitting on the stage waiting for my turn. My palms were sweating, and **my heart was beating like a drum.** I had practiced for weeks, but I worried that I would suddenly forget all of the words I had studied.

1. Determine the meaning of the bolded phrase above.
   A. The author is very excited.
   B. The author is feeling sick.
   C. The author isn't prepared for the spelling bee.
   D. The author is nervous.

2. Josie was so sleepy and bored that she **dozed off** right there on the couch.
   What is the meaning of the bolded phrase above?

   _____

   _____

   _____

3. Benny was very careful as he walked across the old bridge. He knew that if he made one wrong move, he would **plunge** straight down into the water below.
   What detail(s) in the text above helps the reader know the meaning of the word **plunge?**

   _____

   _____

   _____

4. We all have challenges in life. We all have our mountains to climb. For me, it's math class. Math isn't easy for me. But I know if I work hard and keep trying, I'll make it to the top one day.
   What does the author compare his struggles in math class to?

   _____

   _____

   _____

5. Liz was so **swift** that she won every race at school, and it was never even close.
   What does the word **swift** mean in the above sentence?
   - **A.** Fast
   - **B.** Athletic
   - **C.** Clever
   - **D.** Brave

6. After we kicked the soccer ball into Old Man Frank's yard, almost everyone was too scared to go and get it. But not Peter. He walked right into the mean man's yard. Peter had **nerves of steel.**
   What does the phrase **nerves of steel** mean in the sentence above?
   - **A.** Determination
   - **B.** Patience
   - **C.** Courage
   - **D.** Kindness

7. Peter walked into the backyard, and we couldn't see him anymore. We anxiously looked at one another, worried about what would happen next. We all **caught our breath** and listened for the sound of Old Man Frank yelling. At first, we didn't hear anything.
   What detail in the text above helps the reader know what the phrase **caught our breath** means?
   - **A.** "Peter walked into the backyard…"
   - **B.** "…and listened for the sound of Old Man Frank yelling."
   - **C.** "…and we couldn't see him anymore."
   - **D.** "…worried about what would happen next."

8. But soon, we heard it: Old Man Frank. Except he wasn't yelling. He was just talking to Peter, asking him questions like, "How often do you boys play soccer?" He even told Peter a story about when he played soccer as a young boy. Maybe all of our **assumptions** about Old Man Frank had been wrong. It seemed like he wasn't so scary after all.
   What are two details in the text above that help you to understand the meaning of the word **assumptions**?

   _____

   _____

   _____

   _____

IDENTIFY & UNDERSTAND PARTS OF TEXTS

RL.2.5 Refer to parts of stories, dramas, and poems when writing or speaking about a text, using terms such as chapter, scene, and stanza; describe how each successive part builds on earlier sections.

Directions: Answer the questions below.

1. A paragraph is to a story like a stanza is to _____.
   A. A topic
   B. A poem
   C. An illustration
   D. Words

2. A paragraph is to a story like a _____ is to a play.
   A. Stanza
   B. Scene
   C. Character
   D. Text Feature

3. What is the main purpose of line breaks in a poem?
   A. To organize the poem into chapters.
   B. To help the reader read with emotion.
   C. To enhance ideas and meaning.
   D. To let the reader take a breath.

4. When does the author usually introduce the characters and describe the setting in a story? Explain why.

   _____

   _____

   _____

   _____

5. When is a story's problem usually solved? Explain why.

   _____

   _____

   _____

The Sheep
Ann and Jane Taylor

Directions: Read the poem and answer the questions that follow.

1   "Lazy sheep, pray tell me why
In the pleasant fields you lie,
Eating grass, and daisies white,
From the morning till the night?
Everything can something do,
But what kind of use are you?"

2   "Nay, my little master, nay,
Do not serve me so, I pray;
Don't you see the wool that grows
On my back, to make you clothes?
Cold, and very cold, you'd be
If you had not wool from me.

3   True, it seems a pleasant thing,
To nip the daisies in the spring;
But many chilly nights I pass
On the cold and dewy grass,
Or pick a scanty dinner, where
All the common's brown and bare.

4   Then the farmer comes at last,
When the merry spring is past,
And cuts my woolly coat away,
To warm you in the winter's day:
Little master, this is why
In the pleasant fields I lie."

6. How many stanzas does this poem have?
     A. 5
     B. 4
     C. 10
     D. 16

7. Which lines describe best why the master should appreciate the sheep?

A. True, it seems a pleasant thing,
To nip the daisies in the spring;

B. But many chilly nights I pass
On the cold and dewy grass,

C. Don't you see the wool that grows
On my back, to make you clothes?

D. Everything can something do,
But what kind of use are you?"

8. Read these lines from the poem:

Then the farmer comes at last,
When the merry spring is past,
And cuts my woolly coat away,
To warm you in the winter's day:

Why do you think the author included this information?

A. To help readers imagine how a woolly coat can keep them warm.
B. To show that the main benefit of owning a sheep comes in winter, not spring.
C. To show that winter will soon arrive.
D. To suggest that the farmer would like a woolly coat.

IDENTIFY POINT OF VIEW OF SELF & AUTHOR/CHARACTERS

RL.2.6 Student should be able to distinguish own point of view from that of the narrator or those of the characters.

Directions: Answer the questions below.

1. What is a story's point of view?
    A. How the characters are introduced.
    B. The story's lesson or moral.
    C. Who is narrating or telling the story.
    D. The problem that must be solved in the story.

2. What is a third-person point of view?
    A. When a character in the story is the narrator and uses words like I, me, and we.
    B. When the narrator is not part of the story and uses words like he, she, and they.
    C. When there is only one character in the story.
    D. When the main character is the first person mentioned in the story.

Directions: Read the passage below and answer the questions.

Home at Last

1   It was cold and rainy outside, but I had nowhere to go. I hid under some bushes to try to shield myself from the rain.

2   Later, I tried to run across the street to find better shelter. Drivers honked angrily as their cars almost hit me. "Get out of the way!" someone yelled.

3   The rain was slowing down, but now I was hungry. I walked around looking for food. Someone threw a bread crust on the sidewalk, so I ran over to eat it. "Get lost!" a man yelled as I walked across his path.

4   But then another man saw me and bent down, smiling. "Hi, little puppy," he said. "Aren't you cute?"

5   It was the first time someone had been nice to me in days. I wagged my tail happily.

6   "Are you lost?" he asked. "Do you have anywhere to go?"

7   I wanted to explain to the man that I didn't have a home, but he seemed to understand anyway. "Do you want to come home with me?" he asked.

8   I wagged my tail again. The man picked me up, put me in his car, and drove me to his house.

9   "A dog?" asked his wife. "Are you crazy? We don't need a dog."

10   I was scared that I would have to go back outside, but the man asked his wife, "Please, Susie?" The woman agreed, but she didn't look very happy.

3. This question has two parts. First, answer Part A. Then, answer Part B.
Part A
Who is the narrator of this story?
>   **A.** A man
>   **B.** A woman
>   **C.** A puppy
>   **D.** A young boy

Part B
What character in the story gives the reader insight as to the narrator's identity?
>   **A.** The man who yells, "Get out of the way!"
>   **B.** The man who brings the puppy home.
>   **C.** The woman
>   **D.** The rain

4.   From what point of view is this story written?
>   **A.** First person
>   **B.** Second person
>   **C.** Third person
>   **D.** Fourth person

5.   What does the author do to make you feel bad for the puppy? Use details from the passage to support your answer.

_____

_____

_____

_____

_____

6. What is the feeling of the narrator at the beginning of this story?
>   **A.** Happy
>   **B.** Bored
>   **C.** Cold
>   **D.** Tired

7. This question has two parts. First, answer Part A. Then, answer Part B.

Part A

What detail in the story best shows the woman's point of view about the dog?

    A. "The woman agreed..."

    B. "...but she didn't look very happy."

    C. "I was scared that I would have to go back outside."

    D. "The man asked his wife, 'Please, Susie?'"

Part B

What information about the dog might change the woman's point of view?

    A. The dog is homeless.

    B. The dog needs a bath.

    C. The dog has fleas.

    D. The dog is scared of humans.

8. How do the other human characters in the story have a different point of view than the man who takes the dog home? Use details from the story to support your response.

_____

_____

_____

_____

_____

_____

_____

_____

IDENTIFY HOW ILLUSTRATIONS CONVEY INFORMATION

RL.3.7 Explain how specific aspects of a text's illustrations contribute to what is conveyed by the words in a story (e.g., create mood, emphasize aspects of a character or setting).

Directions: Read the text and observe the images below, then answer the questions.

Passage 1: The First Day of School

Nathan and Julie were twins and best friends. They never got to be in the same class, but third grade was different. This year, Nathan and Julie had the same teacher!

The twins had just gotten home from the first day of third grade, and all they could talk about was how nice their new teacher seemed. Most of their best friends were also in the same class.

Some of the topics they would be learning about seemed a little challenging, but Nathan and Julie were confident that third grade would be a good year.

1. What do you think is happening in this picture? Why?

_____

_____

_____

_____

2. How do the characters (Nathan and Julie) feel in this picture? Why do you think so? Use evidence from both the text and the pictures to support your response.

_____

_____

_____

_____

3. What clues does the author give you to show you that Nathan and Julie are confident that third grade will be a great year? Use at least one piece of evidence from both the text and the pictures to support your response.

_____

_____

_____

_____

Passage 2: My Giant Dog

I have the friendliest, sweetest dog in the world. He's also enormous. My dog is so big that a lot of people think he's scary or mean.

But his heart is just as big as the rest of him. Whenever I'm feeling sad, he notices and comes to cuddle with me. He walks my little brother and me to the school bus every morning to make sure we're safe. When we get home from school, he greets us enthusiastically, wagging his tail and trying to lick us. I can't imagine a better dog. My older sister even taught him to dance!

From my giant dog, I've learned not to judge others based on their appearance. My dog may be a giant, but he's not mean or scary.

4. What physical characteristic about the dog does this image emphasize?
   A. The dog is hungry
   B. The dog is enormous.
   C. The dog is cute.
   D. The dog is funny.

5. What character trait of the dog's does this image emphasize?
   A. He's mean.
   B. He's scary and intimidating.
   C. He's scared.
   D. He's sweet and loving.

6. What is the purpose of the image above? How does it add to the information in the text?

_____

_____

_____

7. Look at the image below.

How do you think the boy is feeling in the picture above? Explain why.

_____

_____

_____

_____

_____

_____

COMPARE & CONTRAST NARRATIVES

RL.3.9 Compare and contrast the themes, settings, and plots of stories written by the same author about the same or similar characters (e.g., in books from a series).

Directions: Read the passages below and answer the questions.

Passage 1: The Goose and the Golden Egg
Adapted from the fable by Aesop

1   There was once a farmer who owned a golden goose. Every day, the goose laid a beautiful, shiny golden egg.

2   People came from far and wide to see the magnificent goose and her golden eggs. The farmer began taking the eggs to market, and people would pay large amounts of money to buy them.

3   The farmer was getting richer than he had ever imagined. But he wanted more. The goose only gave the farmer one egg each day, and the farmer decided this was not enough. He became impatient with the goose.

4   One day, the farmer was counting his money when an idea came to him. If he cut the goose open, he could get all of the golden eggs at once. That way, he wouldn't have to wait for one egg each day, and he could make much more money.

5   Imagining what he would do with his riches, the farmer cut the goose. To his disappointment, he didn't find even one golden egg inside. His plan had failed!

6   And now the farmer's precious golden goose was dead. He would never lay another golden egg.

Passage 2: The Dog and His Reflection
Adapted from the fable by Aesop

1   One day, a dog was running past the butcher's shop. The butcher threw the dog a bone. The excited dog began hurrying home with his delicious prize.

2   As the dog was crossing a bridge, he looked down and saw his reflection in the water. But the dog didn't realize that he was looking at his reflection. Instead, he

thought he was looking at another dog. And he thought the other dog had a much bigger bone in his mouth!

3   If the dog had stopped to think for a minute, he might have realized his mistake. But instead of thinking, he dropped his bone and jumped at the dog in the river. He was hoping to take the bigger bone for himself.

4   Instead of getting a bone, the dog found himself having to swim frantically to shore. He finally reached the shore and dragged himself out of the water.

5   Now instead of having a bigger bone, the dog had no bone at all. He stood on the shore, thinking sadly about the delicious bone he had lost.

1. How are the farmer and the dog alike in these two stories? Use details from the passages to support your response.

_____

_____

_____

_____

_____

_____

_____

2. This question has two parts. First, answer Part A. Then, answer Part B.
Part A
What is the setting of the first passage?

    A. A river

    B. A farm

    C. A mountain

    D. A school

Part B
What is the setting of the second passage?

    A. A river

    B. A farm

    C. A mountain

    D. A school

3. This question has two parts. First, answer Part A. Then, answer Part B.

Part A

Which of the following could be a theme of both stories?

    A. Make good choices.

    B. Be careful who you trust.

    C. Treat others the way that you want to be treated.

    D. Be grateful for what you have instead of being greedy.

Part B

What detail from the first passage helps develop this theme?

    A. "People came from far and wide to see the magnificent goose and her golden eggs." (Paragraph 2)

    B. "The farmer was getting richer than he had ever imagined." (Paragraph 3)

    C. "The farmer was counting his money when an idea came to him." (Paragraph 4)

    D. "And now the farmer's precious golden goose was dead. He would never lay another golden egg." (Paragraph 6)

4. What decision do the characters make in Passage 1 and in Passage 2, and what are the results?

The farmer's decision:

_____

_____

The result:

_____

_____

_____

The dog's decision:

_____

_____

The result:

_____

_____

_____

5. What is the problem in both stories?
   A. The main characters want more than what they have.
   B. Other characters try to take what the main characters have.
   C. The main characters both get lost.
   D. The main characters don't have enough money to buy something important.

6. What caused the farmer to cut open his goose? Use details from the story to support your answer.

   _____

   _____

   _____

   _____

7. Why did the dog jump into the river? Use details from the story to support your answer.

   _____

   _____

   _____

   _____

8. Select the sentences below that show how the farmer and the dog are different
   ☐ The farmer wants more money, while the dog wants a bigger bone.
   ☐ The farmer mistakenly thinks he can get more eggs if he cuts open the goose, while the dog mistakenly thinks his reflection is another dog with a bigger bone.
   ☐ The dog loses his bone and the farmer accidentally kills his goose.
   ☐ A farmer gave the dog a bone, while the farmer gets his golden goose from the market
   ☐ The dog's story takes place on a river, while the farmer's story takes place on a farm.
   ☐ The farmer is happy at the end of the story, while the dog is scared at the end of the story.

READING: INFORMATION

ASK & ANSWER QUESTIONS USING TEXT EVIDENCE

RI.1.1 Ask and answer questions to demonstrate understanding of a text, referring explicitly to the text as the basis for the answers.

Directions: Read the passage and answer the questions that follow.

Passage 1: About the Starfish

1   Marine scientists are trying to change the name "starfish" to "sea star" because the name isn't accurate. Why? The starfish is not a fish.

2   Like fish, the starfish does live underwater. However, it doesn't have scales, gills, or fins. It can only live in saltwater. The starfish is actually an echinoderm, like sand dollars and sea urchins.

3   Around the world, there are about 2,000 different species of starfish. Most of them have five arms, but some have 10 arms, 20 arms, or even 40 arms. They have hard, bony skin that can protect them from predators. Most of them also have bright colors that can scare off predators or be used as camouflage to hide from predators.

4   Starfish, or sea stars, are very unique animals. They have one eye on the tip of each arm, and their eyes can't see color. They don't have brains or blood. Instead of blood, starfish have sea water running through their bodies.

5   If a starfish loses an arm, they have the amazing ability to make it grow back. Some species can even grow a whole new sea star from a broken arm.

1. The name "starfish" is not accurate because the starfish
    A. does not look like a star.
    B. is not a fish.
    C. doesn't live underwater.
    D. has scales, but not fins or gills.

2. Which of the following is NOT a way that starfish protect themselves from predators?
    A. Their skin is hard and bony.
    B. They use their bright colors to scare predators.
    C. They have sharp spikes on each arm.
    D. They also use their bright colors as camouflage to hide from predators.

3. List three things that make the starfish a unique animal.

    1. _____

    2. _____

    3. _____

4. How many arms does the starfish have? Use evidence from the text to support your answer.

    _____

    _____

    _____

    _____

    _____

    _____

    _____

Passage 2: The Starfish Killer

1   Back in 2012, millions of starfish started dying out across North America. A mysterious starfish killer turned these sea stars into piles of "white goo" or "white slime."

2   Recently, scientists have discovered exactly what has been killing starfish. It's a type of parvovirus. The virus causes starfish to become weak, and it leaves them open to bacterial infections. The bacterial infection kills the starfish.

3   About 8-17 days after infection, the starfish starts to develop white sores on its body. Sometimes, the starfish's arms rip off and walk away. Eventually, the starfish melts into a pile of white goo.

4   This virus isn't new, but scientists aren't sure what's causing it to kill so many starfish. In the past, the virus only attacked one or two species at a time. Now, over 20 species of starfish have been affected, including the sunflower star, the giant pink star, and the rainbow star.

5   Some scientists think the virus is spreading so quickly because there are so many sea stars packed into small areas.

6   Scientists are continuing to study this parvovirus to see if they can stop it. If they can't stop it, scientists hope to be able to prevent it from happening again in the future.

5.   Using details from the passage, complete the sequence of events below.

     (1) The starfish catches the parvovirus.

     (2) _____

     (3) The starfish gets a bacterial infection.

     (4) _____

     (5) _____

     (6) The starfish melts into a pile of white goo.

6.   Where is the parvovirus mostly killing starfish?
     A. North America
     B. Around the world
     C. Asia
     D. The Caribbean

7. The following question has two parts. First, answer Part A. Then, answer Part B.

Part A

The parvovirus isn't new. But what is different about the virus nowadays?

  A. It's affecting starfish all over the world.

  B. It's affecting many different species of starfish.

  C. It's turning starfish to white goo.

  D. It's killing starfish in days instead of weeks.

Part B

What do scientists think the reason is for the change in Part A?

  A. The virus is growing more powerful.

  B. Starfish aren't as strong as they were in the past.

  C. There are large numbers of starfish packed into small areas.

  D. This is a different type of parvovirus.

8. Based on the details in the passage, what inference can be made about how scientists will respond to the parvovirus? Use details from the passage to support your answer.

_____

_____

_____

_____

_____

_____

_____

DETERMINE MAIN IDEA & EXPLAIN KEY DETAILS

RI.1.2 Determine the main idea of a text; recount the key details and explain how they support the main idea.

Directions: Read the passage and answer the questions that follow.

Passage 1: The Invention of the Potato Chip

1   Have you ever eaten a potato chip and wondered how this salty treat was invented? Maybe through lots of time, effort, and experimenting?

2   Actually, the answer might surprise you. The potato chip was invented completely by accident. A hotel chef named George Crum cooked some fried potatoes for his customers. But the customers thought George's fried potatoes were disgusting. They complained that the potatoes were too thick and too bland, or flavorless.

3   George Crum was furious that the customers had complained about his food. He decided to teach them a lesson. George grabbed some more potatoes and sliced them until they were as thin as a piece of paper. Next, he put an excessive amount of salt on them.

4   George was sure that the customers would think that these fried potatoes were even worse, and they would learn to appreciate his delicious food.

5   Instead, the customers loved the new fried potatoes! Soon, everyone was talking about the tasty potato chips that George Crum had invented.

6   So next time you eat a bag of potato chips, remember that it all started with a hotel chef trying to prank his rude customers.

1. Select the statement that describes the main idea of the article.
    A. George Crum was not a very nice chef.
    B. Potato chips were invented by accident.
    C. Customers should be polite, not rude.
    D. Sometimes our plans don't go the way we expect.

2. List at least two details that support the main idea.

_____

_____

_____

3. Which quote from the passage best supports the main idea?

    A. "George Crum was furious that the customers had complained about his food." (Paragraph 3)

    B. "They complained that the potatoes were too thick and too bland, or flavorless." (Paragraph 2)

    C. "So next time you eat a bag of potato chips, remember that it all started with a hotel chef trying to prank his customers." (Paragraph 6)

    D. "Instead, the customers loved the new fried potatoes!" (Paragraph 5)

4. What is another title that could be used for this passage?

    A. The Rude Customers

    B. The Angry Chef

    C. Hotel Cooking Adventures

    D. Potato Chips: A Happy Accident

Passage 2: The Invention of Baseball

1   Until 2011, popular legend was that a man named Abner Doubleday invented the sport of baseball. Abner Doubleday was a man who eventually fired one of the first shots in the Civil War, and he became a heroic general.

2   According to the legend, 20-year-old Doubleday invented the sport in 1839 in Cooperstown, New York. He used a stick to draw his idea for baseball in the dirt. It was a new game he had invented that he and his friends could play.

3   The story was so popular that the National Baseball Hall of Fame was opened in Cooperstown, New York, where baseball was supposedly invented.

4   But the truth is that Doubleday did not invent baseball. Major League Baseball's historian, John Thorn, published a book explaining that baseball was played long before 1839. As early as the 1800's, different versions of baseball were played in New York, Philadelphia, and Massachusetts. A similar bat and ball game, called Rounders, was also played in Britain.

5   So who did invent baseball? Historian John Thorn says that this is one question that will probably never be answered.

5. Which of the following best describes the main idea of this passage?
   A. Despite the popular legend that Abner Doubleday invented baseball, we don't know who actually invented the sport.
   B. Different versions of baseball were played in New York, Philadelphia, Massachusetts, and even Britain.
   C. According to legend, 20-year-old Abner Doubleday invented the sport of baseball in Cooperstown, New York in 1839.
   D. John Thorn published a book explaining that Abner Doubleday did not invent baseball, because baseball was being played long before 1839.

6. List at least two details that support or develop the main idea.

----

7. Which of the following quotes does NOT support the main idea of this passage?

    A. "As early as the 1800's, different versions of baseball were played in New York, Philadelphia, and Massachusetts." (Paragraph 4)

    B. "The story was so popular that the National Baseball Hall of Fame was opened in Cooperstown, New York, where baseball was supposedly invented." (Paragraph 3)

    C. "But the truth is that Doubleday did not invent baseball." (Paragraph 4)

    D. "Abner Doubleday was a man who eventually fired one of the first shots in the Civil War, and he became a heroic general." (Paragraph 1)

8. Who invented baseball?

    A. Abner Doubleday

    B. John Thorn

    C. We'll probably never know.

    D. Someone in Britain who called the game "Rounders."

DESCRIBE & UNDERSTAND RELATIONSHIPS BETWEEN IDEAS

RI.3.3 Describe the relationship between a series of historical events, scientific ideas or concepts, or steps in technical procedures in a text, using language that pertains to time, sequence, and cause/effect.

Directions: Read the passage and answer the questions that follow.

Passage 1: The Sinking of The Titanic

1   On April 15, 1912, a huge steamship called the Titanic hit an iceberg and sank to the bottom of the Atlantic Ocean. Over 1,500 people drowned in the tragic accident. It was the very first time the Titanic had sailed.

2   At the time, the Titanic was the largest ship that had ever been built. It had a swimming pool, a gym, several cafes, a library, a barber shop, and more. People believed it was "the safest ship ever."

3   Because people thought the ship was unsinkable, there were only 20 lifeboats on board. This was enough to hold only half of the passengers and crew. Nothing bad could happen to the Titanic, people thought. But when something bad did happen, there weren't enough lifeboats to get everyone to safety.

4   The Titanic also received at least five warnings that there was ice ahead, but the warnings were ignored. Some historians say that the captain, Edward J. Smith, was trying to cross the Atlantic faster than another ship, the Olympic. For an icy area, the Titanic was traveling way too fast.

5   If the ship had been moving slower, they might have seen the iceberg in time. The ship also might have hit the iceberg with less force and caused less damage.

1. Why were there only 20 lifeboats on board the Titanic?
    A. 20 was the correct number of lifeboats for a ship that size.
    B. People thought that the Titanic was unsinkable.
    C. It was too expensive to buy more lifeboats.
    D. 20 lifeboats would hold all of the passengers and crew.

2. Why do many historians believes the Titanic was traveling so fast?
    A. The captain wanted to beat the speed of another ship.
    B. They were trying to get away from the icebergs.
    C. There was a storm coming, and the captain wanted to beat it.
    D. The Titanic was traveling the appropriate speed.

3. What are two factors that made the Titanic accident worse? Use evidence from the text to support your response.

_____

_____

_____

_____

_____

_____

_____

4. How did people's beliefs about the Titanic affect what happened to the ship? Use details from the text to support your answer.

_____

_____

_____

_____

_____

_____

_____

Passage 2: The Great Chicago Fire

1   In 1871, almost the entire city of Chicago was made of wood. There were wooden buildings, wooden sidewalks, and even wooden streets. Therefore, it's no surprise that the Great Chicago Fire of October 8, 1871 spread quickly and caused major damage.

2   The week before the Great Chicago Fire, there were 20 fires in the city. The firefighters were exhausted when they got a call on October 8th around 9:00 PM that a fire had started behind the O'Leary home. Catherine and Patrick O'Leary lived in the home with their five children.

3   At first, the firefighters were sent to the wrong neighborhood. By the time they finally got to the O'Leary house, the fire was out of control. The fire continued to burn for two days until rain fell and extinguished it. Thousands of buildings burnt down, and hundreds of people died in the fire.

4   Mrs. O'Leary explained to reporters that she was sleeping when the fire started. But newspapers reported that she was milking her cow in the barn and the cow kicked over a lantern, starting the terrible fire. Almost everyone in Chicago blamed Mrs. O'Leary for the destructive fire. After the fire, everyone was so angry with Mrs. O'Leary that she stayed in her house and avoided other people.

5   Architects rebuilt Chicago with the world's first skyscrapers. The population and the economy grew, and Chicago became a great city again.

5. List at least two reasons that the Great Chicago Fire spread so quickly.

_____

_____

_____

_____

_____

_____

6. Why was the fire out of control by the time the firefighters got to the O'Leary house?
    A. Mrs. O'Leary was sleeping when the fire started.
    B. Mrs. O'Leary's cow had kicked over the lantern.
    C. The firefighters were sent to the wrong neighborhood first.
    D. The firefighters were sleeping and took too long to get to the house.

7. Who or what did the people of Chicago blame for the fire?

    A. The wooden buildings, sidewalks, and streets

    B. Mrs. O'Leary and her cow

    C. The exhausted firefighters who went to the wrong neighborhood

    D. Mrs. O'Leary's five children

8. What was one positive effect of the Chicago Fire? Use details from the passage to support your response.

_____

_____

_____

_____

9. How did the Chicago Fire change Mrs. O'Leary's life? Use details from the passage to support your answer.

_____

_____

_____

_____

10. What finally stopped The Great Chicago Fire?

    A. The Chicago firefighters

    B. The rain

    C. A team of volunteers

    D. Firefighters from neighboring cities

11. How are Passage 1 (The Sinking of the Titanic) and Passage 2 (The Great Chicago Fire) similar? Be sure to use at least 1 detail from each passage to support your answer.

_____

_____

_____

_____

_____

_____

_____

DETERMINE DOMAIN-SPECIFIC WORD MEANING IN CONTEXT

RI.2.4 Determine the meaning of general academic and domain-specific words and phrases in a text relevant to a grade 3 topic or subject area.

Directions: Read the passage and answer the questions that follow.

Passage 1: The Cactus Plant

1   The cactus is a type of plant known as a succulent. It can store water to drink later if it doesn't rain for a long time. Cacti (more than one cactus plant) can store water in their stems, roots, and leaves. In fact, a cactus plant can live for an entire year without rain.

2   How does the cactus plant store so much water? Its spikes, which are actually called spines, help prevent the water from escaping. The cactus plant's waxy skin helps it hold in water too.

3   When you envision a cactus plant, you probably picture a spiky green plant. Actually, there are about 2,000 different types of cacti. Most are green, but some have a bluish or brownish hue. Some are flat and some are round, and they come in many unique shapes. They also grow large flowers that can be yellow, red, pink, white, orange, or blue. Some cacti even grow fruit.

4   Cacti do grow mostly in the desert or in other dry areas because they require dry, rocky soil. However, some cacti have been found in rainforests or as far north as Canada.

5   Cactus plants are most prevalent in Arizona, California, and Texas. People visit from all over just to see the many cacti that grow in these states, especially when the flowers are blooming between the months of March and May.

1. What is the meaning of the underlined word as it is used in this sentence from the passage?

    Cactus plants are most <u>prevalent</u> in Arizona, California, and Texas. (Paragraph 5)
    A. common
    B. beautiful
    C. large
    D. opular

2. What is a succulent? Use details from the passage to support your answer.

_____

_____

_____

_____

_____

_____

_____

3. What is the meaning of the underlined word as it is used in this sentence from the passage?

   Most are green, but some have a greenish or brownish <u>hue.</u> (Paragraph 3)
   A. flower
   B. color
   C. fruit
   D. skin

4. What is the meaning of the underlined word as it is used in this sentence from the passage?

   When you <u>envision</u> a cactus plant, you probably picture a spiky green plant. (Paragraph 3)
   A. see
   B. describe
   C. draw
   D. imagine

Passage 2: The Cocoa Bean

1   If you've ever enjoyed a chocolate bar, chocolate cake, or chocolate ice cream, then you've eaten cocoa beans. Cocoa beans grow on trees in tropical climates, and they're used to make chocolate.

2   Cocoa trees only grow close to the Equator because they need hot and somewhat wet weather to flourish. The trees also need shade to grow, so they usually grow in the shade of other plants, such as mango and papaya trees.

3   Cocoa trees produce orange fruit, called pods. The pods have seeds on the inside, and these seeds are what we call cocoa beans. The beans are a milky white color at first, and they would taste extremely bitter if you ate them right off the tree.

4   To transform these bitter cocoa beans into delicious chocolate, chocolatiers have to first dry out the beans. Once the beans are dry, they become brownish-red in color. They're then transported to a chocolate factory, where the beans are roasted.

5   The roasted cocoa beans are chopped into pieces called cocoa nibs. Heat and pressure are used to extract two liquids from the cocoa nibs: cocoa liquor and cocoa butter. These two liquids are mixed with sugar and milk powder, and we finally have the finished product!

6   The chocolate is sometimes poured into molds to give it a candy bar shape, then wrapped by a machine, and eventually placed on a shelf and purchased by kids like you. Who knew your favorite treat took such a journey to get to you?

5. What is a <u>chocolatier</u> (Paragraph 4)? Use evidence from the text to support your answer.

_____

_____

_____

6. What does the author mean by the underlined phrase in this sentence from the passage?

These two liquids are mixed with sugar and milk powder, and we finally have <u>the finished product!</u> (Paragraph 5)
   A. Cocoa beans
   B. Cocoa nibs
   C. Chocolate
   D. Candy bars

7. What is the meaning of the underlined word as it used in this sentence from the passage?

    Heat and pressure are used to <u>extract</u> two liquids from the cocoa nibs: cocoa liquor and cocoa butter. (Paragraph 5)
    - **A.** make
    - **B.** remove
    - **C.** mix
    - **D.** carry

8. Select the **TWO** correct meanings of the word <u>journey</u> as it is used in the sentence.

    Who knew your favorite chocolate bar took such a <u>journey</u> to get to you? (Paragraph 6)
    - **A.** Traveling from one place to another
    - **B.** A fun trip or vacation
    - **C.** A long process
    - **D.** Hard work
    - **E.** Ocean voyage

USE TEXT FEATURES & SEARCH TOOLS

RI.2.5 Use text features and search tools (e.g., key words, sidebars, hyperlinks) to locate information relevant to a given topic efficiently.

Directions: Read the passage and answer the questions that follow.

Passage 1: Caves

1   A cave is a space under the surface of the Earth, in cliff walls, or in hillsides. Many times, caves are a complicated system of connected underground passageways, kind of like a maze.

Types of Caves

2   Caves form over a long period of time, because the processes that make caves are very slow. There are several different processes that can make caves, and they form different types of caves.

3   **Solutional caves** are the most common, and they are formed from rainfall and chemical processes. The acid in the water eats away at the rock surface below, making a hole. The hole gets larger and larger, and eventually forms a cave.

4   Caves are also formed when hot lava from a volcano melts the rock surface below, making a hole.

5   **Sea caves** are formed when sea cliffs are eroded by waves and tides. The eroded cliff eventually forms a cave.

Cave Features

6   Rock formations decorate most caves. These formations can hang down from the ceiling, sprout up from the ground, or cover the sides of a cave.

7   The most common formations are **stalactites** and **stalagmites**. Rock formations that hang from the ceiling are called stalactites. Rock formations that sprout up from the ground are called stalagmites. Both of these are formed from dripping water.

Cave Creatures

8   Some animals like to spend time in cave entrances, but they don't live inside of caves. For example, foxes, bears, spiders, cockroaches, bats and frogs all like to take up shelter at cave entrances. Some birds may also build nests in cave entrances.

9   However, there are some animals that truly live in caves and these animals never go outside. Scientists who study caves, called **speleologists**, believe there are around 50,000 different species of animals that live in caves, and we will probably never discover them all.

1. What is the purpose of the headings in this passage?
   A. To tell the reader the author's opinion
   B. To help the reader visualize information
   C. To help the reader find the main idea of each section
   D. To help the reader place events in order

2. Why are some of the words in the paragraphs in bold text?
   A. To point out the main idea of the whole passage
   B. To draw the reader's attention to an important word
   C. To make the text look nice and easy to read
   D. To help the reader visualize information

3. What information can be found under the heading "Cave Features?"
   A. Caves are also formed when hot lava from a volcano melts the rock surface below.
   B. Some animals like to spend time in cave entrances but don't live in caves.
   C. Caves often hold a complicated system of connected underground passageways, kind of like a maze.
   D. Formations that hang from the ceiling are called stalactites.

4. Under which heading could the following information be added?

   "Technically, bats do not truly live in caves. This is because they sleep in caves, but they leave often to hunt for food."
   A. Cave Features
   B. Cave Creatures
   C. Types of Caves
   D. A new heading

5. Select the type text feature in the article that explains the difference between solutional caves and sea caves.
   A. Paragraphs
   B. Annotations
   C. Headings
   D. Subtitles

6. This question has two parts. First, answer Part A. Then, answer Part B.

Part A

What is a sea cave?

    A. A cave formed from rainfall and chemical processes.

    B. A cave formed by an erupting volcano.

    C. A rock formation formed from dripping water.

    D. A cave formed when sea cliffs are eroded by waves and tides.

Part B

Select the **TWO** text features you were able to use to find this information quickly.

    A. Footnote

    B. Headings

    C. Bold text

    D. Glossary

    E. Dictionary

7. If you wanted to search online for more information about the different types of caves, what words could you use to start your search?

    A. Solutional caves

    B. Cave features

    C. Animals that live in caves

    D. Cave Types

8. If the article included an alphabetical list of the bold words, along with their definitions, it would be called a/an:

    A. Glossary

    B. Index

    C. Hyperlink

    D. Caption

IDENTIFY POINT OF VIEW OF SELF & AUTHOR

RI.2.6 Distinguish their own point of view from that of the author of a text.

Directions: Read the passage and answer the questions that follow.

Passage 1: The Importance of Exercise

1   You probably know that exercise can make you strong and healthy, but being active might have more benefits than you realize.

2   Exercising regularly can help people maintain a healthy weight and prevent diseases like diabetes and high blood pressure. But it can also benefit your mind! Exercise produces endorphins, which are chemicals that help people feel happy and relaxed. And the more you exercise, the better your body and mind can handle situations that might make you feel stressed or anxious.

3   Exercising can also help people sleep better at night. Many people who exercise regularly feel more confident and energetic too.

4   Getting benefits from exercise doesn't require going to the gym every day or working out for hours. Just 30 minutes of physical activity can be extremely helpful. You can play a sport or a game with friends, go for a jog, ride a bike, dance, or even walk your dog. Just get up and move for 30 minutes a day, and you'll see wonderful benefits for your body and your mind.

1.   Select the **TWO** sentences from the passage that best help you understand the author's point of view.

☐ "Just get up and move for 30 minutes a day, and you'll see wonderful benefits for your body and mind." (Paragraph 4)

☐ "Exercising can help people sleep better at night." (Paragraph 3)

☐ "You probably know that exercise can make you strong and healthy, but being active might have more benefits than you realize." (Paragraph 1)

☐ "You can play a sport or a game with friends, go for a jog, ride a bike, dance, or even walk your dog." (Paragraph 4)

2. This question has two parts. First, answer Part A. Then, answer Part B.

Part A

Based on the information in the passage, with which statement would the author most likely agree?

A. Eating vegetables is also extremely important.

B. Kids should spend more time outdoors.

C. Exercise is important for physical and mental health.

D. Everyone should go to the gym and exercise.

Part B

Which piece of evidence from the passage supports your answer in Part A?

A. "Exercising regularly can help people maintain a healthy weight…" (Paragraph 2)

B. "Getting benefits from exercise doesn't require going to the gym every day or working out for hours.

C. "You can play a sport or game with your friends, go for a jog, ride a bike, dance, or even walk your dog." (Paragraph 4)

D. "Exercising regularly can help people maintain a healthy weight and prevent diseases like diabetes and high blood pressure. But it can also benefit your mind!" (Paragraph 2)

3. Based on the information in the passage, do you agree or disagree with the author's point of view? Why? What information in the passage influenced your point of view?

_____

_____

_____

_____

_____

_____

_____

Passage 2: Turn Off the TV

1   Kids today spend plenty of time looking at screens: computer screens, phone screens, and television screens. This isn't always a bad thing, but it should be done in moderation. Too much television, for example, can harm children.

2   Kids who consistently watch more than 4 hours of TV a day are more likely to be overweight and unhealthy. Kids who see violence on TV may be more aggressive. They may also start to believe that the world is a scary place and that something bad will happen to them.

3   Today's TV shows are also filled with bad behavior that can influence children to behave badly themselves. Commercials advertise unhealthy foods and drinks that can lead to an unhealthy lifestyle.

4   Plus, too much time spent watching TV can take time away from other, healthier activities. Kids who watch too much TV may spend less time playing outside, talking to friends and family, and reading or doing homework.

5   It's okay to watch an hour or two of TV a day, but don't overdo it. It can lead to an unhealthy lifestyle, bad behavior, and less time spent on more important activities. Do yourself a favor, and turn off the TV!

4. What is the author's point of view about television?
    A. It's okay to watch an hour or two of TV a day.
    B. Kids who see violence on TV may be more aggressive.
    C. Too much television can harm children.
    D. TV commercials advertise too many unhealthy foods and drinks.

5. What are the best words to show the author's point of view about television?
    A. Don't overdo it
    B. 4 hours of TV a day
    C. The world is a scary place
    D. Do yourself a favor

6. This question has two parts. First, answer Part A. Then, answer Part B.
Part A
    Based on the information in the passage, with which statement would the author most likely agree?
    A. It's best for families to not own televisions.
    B. The television should be off during family dinner.
    C. Activities like reading and spending time with family are healthier than watching television.
    D. All kids who watch too much TV behave badly.

Part B

What piece of evidence from the passage supports your answer in Part A?

A. "Kids who consistently watch more than 4 hours of TV a day are likelier to be overweight and unhealthy." (Paragraph 2)

B. "...too much time spent watching TV can take away from other, healthier activities. Kids who spend too much time watching TV may spend less time playing outside, talking to friends and family, and reading or doing homework." (Paragraph 4)

C. "They may also start to believe that the world is a scary place and that something bad will happen to them." (Paragraph 2)

D. "Today's TV shows are also filled with bad behavior that can influence children to behave badly themselves. Commercials advertise unhealthy foods and drinks that can lead to an unhealthy lifestyle." (Paragraph 3)

7. After reading the information in this passage, do you agree or disagree with the author's point of view? Be sure to use details from the passage to support your answer.

_____

_____

_____

_____

8. How does the title of the article give you information about the author's point of view?

_____

_____

_____

_____

USE & UNDERSTAND INFORMATION IN ILLUSTRATIONS

RI.3.7 Use information gained from illustrations (e.g., maps, photographs) and the words in a text to demonstrate understanding of the text (e.g., where, when, why, and how key events occur).

Directions: Read the passage and answer the questions that follow.

Passage 1: States of Matter

1   Matter is anything that takes up mass and space. In other words, matter is the "stuff" that the universe is made of. Matter is made up of atoms and molecules which combine to make up objects like the desk you're sitting in, the pencil you're holding, the paper you're reading, and even you. Matter exists in three main states (or forms): solids, liquids, and gases.

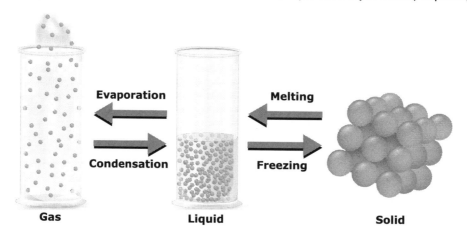

2   The air you're breathing right now is made of gases. Gas molecules are spread out and very energetic. They move around constantly. Gases are mostly invisible and have no fixed shape.

3   If you put a gas inside of a container, it will spread out to fill the whole container, no matter how big or small it is.

4   Liquids include water and soda. They are made up of molecules that aren't as spread out as gas molecules. But they're more spread out than solid molecules.

5   Liquid molecules can also move around easily, although they don't have as much energy as gas molecules. Liquids don't have their own shape. Instead, they take the shape of the container they're in.

6   Solids include you, your desk, your chair, and your friend. Solids are made up of molecules that group closely together and don't move around. Solids do have their own shape. The shape of a solid does not change when it's placed in a container.

7   Objects can sometimes change from one state of matter to another. For example, a liquid can evaporate and become a gas. A solid can melt and become a liquid, like when ice melts and turns into water. A liquid can freeze and become a solid, like when water freezes and becomes ice.

1. Based on the passage and the illustration, which state of matter has the most spread out molecules?
    A. Gas
    B. Liquid
    C. Solid
    D. None. They're all equal.

2. How does the illustration help you better understand the passage?
    A. It corrects information that was wrong in the passage.
    B. It adds information about many more states of matter.
    C. It helps readers see and imagine the information in the passage, and adds new information about the ways that states of matter change.
    D. It makes the passage more fun to read.

3. Which state of matter has its own shape that does not change?
    A. Gas
    B. Liquid
    C. Solid
    D. All of the above.

4. The passage explains that objects can change from one state of matter to another, like when melting causes a solid to become a liquid. The illustration has arrows that show how these changes can happen, including that freezing can cause a _____ to turn into a _____.

5. Based on the information in the illustration, can a liquid turn into a gas? Explain your answer.

    _____

    _____

6. Select the **TWO** types of molecules that move around.
    ☐ Gas
    ☐ Solid
    ☐ Liquid
    ☐ Condensation

Passage 2: Moons of the Solar System

1   Did you know that Earth isn't the only planet with a moon? In fact, some planets have moons that are bigger than Earth's moon. Jupiter, for example, has 69 moons (that we know of), and some of them are massive.

2   Jupiter's four largest moons are Io, Europa, Ganymede, and Callisto. Europa is smaller than our moon, but the other three are larger. These four moons are very different from one another. For instance, Io is covered in volcanoes. Europa's surface is mostly water ice. Callisto is probably the most ancient, and it's covered in craters.

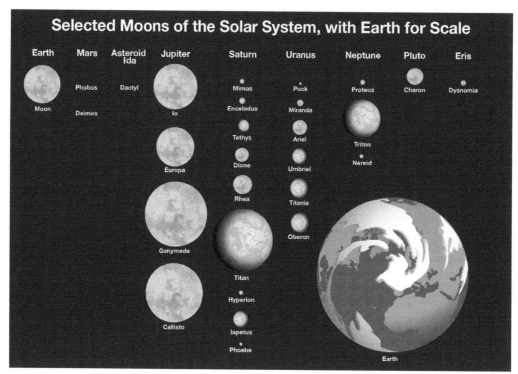

7. Based on the passage and the image, which of Jupiter's four largest moons is NOT bigger than Earth's moon?

    A. Io

    B. Europa

    C. Ganymede

    D. Callisto

8. Based on the image, what other planet has a moon that is much larger than Earth's moon?

    A. Mars

    B. Neptune

    C. Uranus

    D. Saturn

DESCRIBE & MAKE CONNECTIONS IN TEXT

RI.3.8 Describe the logical connection between particular sentences and paragraphs in a text (e.g., comparison, cause/effect, first/second/third in a sequence)

Directions: Read the passage and answer the questions that follow.

Passage 1: One Arm, All Heart

1   Bethany Hamilton was born in Hawaii in 1990. Bethany and her brothers all learned to surf at very young ages. By the young age of eight years old, Bethany Hamilton was a competitive surfer.

2   Bethany was home schooled so that she could pursue her passion of surfing. In 1999, Bethany became sponsored by the Hanalei Surf Company. As a competitor, Bethany was beating people who had been surfing much longer than she had and had much more experience.

3   In October of 2003, Bethany went surfing with her friend Alana, Alana's father, and Alana's brother at Tunnels Beach in Hawaii. Bethany was lying on her surfboard in the ocean when she suddenly felt an intense pressure on her arm while being pulled back and forth. Bethany noticed that the water around her was turning red, but she surprisingly didn't feel any pain. It was her friends who realized that her arm had been split apart almost her shoulder.

4   Eventually, it was determined that Bethany was attacked by a 14-foot tiger shark. As a result of the attack, massive amounts of blood were extravasated from her arm, and Bethany had several surgeries. But, she was discharged from the hospital a few days later.

5   Despite losing her arm, Bethany pledged to get back to surfing as soon as possible. Just one month later, Bethany returned to the waves. In no time, she was back to competing and winning awards. Bethany Hamilton was back and better than ever.

1. Why does the author include the information in Paragraph 2?
    A. To show that Bethany was a poor student
    B. To describe Bethany's passion for surfing
    C. To show Bethany was bad at surfing
    D. To introduce the problem

2. What is the relationship between Paragraph 3 and Paragraph 4?

   A. Paragraph 3 introduces a problem, and Paragraph 4 introduces the solution.

   B. Paragraph 3 shows a cause, and Paragraph 4 shows the effect.

   C. Paragraph 3 introduces a problem, and Paragraph 4 introduces a lesson..

   D. Paragraph 3 introduces the characters and setting, but Paragraph 4 introduces the problem and solution.

3. Why is Paragraph 5 included in the passage? Explain your reasoning using details from the passage.

   _____

   _____

   _____

   _____

   _____

   _____

4. What are the effects of the shark attack? Choose all that apply.

   ☐ Bethany can no longer surf.

   ☐ Bethany undergoes many surgeries.

   ☐ Bethany loses her arm.

   ☐ Bethany has to stay in the hospital for several months.

   ☐ Bethany loses a lot of blood.

   ☐ Bethany makes a promise to herself to return to surfing

READING: INFORMATION

Passage 2: Don't Give Up

1   Patricia Polacco was born on a farm in Michigan in 1944. She lived in Union City, Michigan with her parents and **beloved** grandparents. Patricia grew up in a storytelling family where she heard the most fascinating stories. Her babushka's (grandmother's) stories were some of her favorites.

2   Patricia's parents were divorced when she was just three years old. As a result, Patricia and her brother spent much of their childhood living in two places. They spent the school year in Oakland, California where their mother lived, and they spent the summers in Michigan where their father and grandparents lived.

3   Elementary school was very hard for Patricia. She tried very hard to learn how to read and write, but she just couldn't do it. The harder reading and writing became, the more Patricia concentrated on her drawing. She just loved to draw.

4   Throughout her childhood, Patricia was constantly teased and bullied. Children would call her names like "dumb" and "stupid." She especially hated to read out loud because she always made mistakes, and the teacher had to help her sound out every single word. Eventually, she despised going to school.

5   It wasn't until Patricia was fourteen years old that she learned how to read. One of Patricia's teachers recognized that she had a learning disability called **dyslexia.** Finally, Patricia was able to get the help she needed.

6   Now, Patricia Polacco is a famous writer of children's books. She has written several books such as *Thank You, Mr. Falker* and *The Keeping Quilt.* Many of her books tell about the stories her grandparents told her as a child. Her books also tell about her struggles with learning to read and how she was bullied. Patricia is a wonderful example that if we work hard and never give up, we can **accomplish** great things!

5. Why is it important to mention in Paragraph 3 that school was very hard for Patricia?
    A. The author wanted us to infer that Patricia is a bad student.
    B. The author wanted us to infer that if Patricia tried harder in school, she would have learned how to read.
    C. It gives the reader interesting background information about Patricia.
    D. The author wanted us to understand that even though Patricia tried very hard in school, she still couldn't learn how to read.

6. How does the information in Paragraph 2 build on the information in Paragraph 1?

   A. Paragraph 1 introduces Patricia and Paragraph 2 tells more about her childhood.

   B. Paragraph 1 introduces the cause and Paragraph 2 presents the effect.

   C. Paragraph 2 presents the solution for the problem introduced in Paragraph 1.

   D. Paragraph 1 introduces why Patricia loves stories and Paragraph 2 explains the effect of this.

7. Even though Patricia has a learning disability, she is now a famous author of children's books. What are 2 factors that helped Patricia to become a famous author?

8. Why does the author include Paragraph 4?

   A. To show that Patricia could have learned how to read if she tried harder

   B. To show why Patricia hated school

   C. To explain why Patricia gave up

   D. To show readers that bullying is bad

COMPARE AND CONTRAST KEY POINTS IN TWO TEXTS

RI.3.9 Compare and contrast the most important points and key details presented in two texts on the same topic.

Directions: Read the passages and answer the questions that follow.

Passage 1: Cell Phones Have No Place at School

1   School is a place to learn, and cell phones can prevent students from learning. For this reason, students should not bring cell phones to school.

2   Cell phones cause too much temptation. Students want to see if their friends are texting them, play fun games, watch videos, or check their social media apps. If students decide to look at their phones, they aren't able to pay attention to their assignments or to what the teacher is saying. They may miss important information.

3   Even if students do avoid the temptation to look at their cell phones, they may be distracted by thinking about checking their cell phones or wondering if someone is texting them.

4   Sometimes, students' cell phones go off in the middle of class, which can also be disruptive and distracting. Anything that can interrupt learning has no place in the classroom.

5   Lastly, some students use cell phones to share answers on assignments and tests. They may text each other answers or send one another pictures of assignments. Some students might also use their cell phones to look up answers for assignments and tests. When students cheat, they don't learn the information for themselves. This is another reason that cell phones can prevent kids from doing what they're supposed to be doing at school: learning.

Passage 2: Should Cell Phones Be Allowed at School?

1   Many people disagree on the issue of whether or not cell phones should be allowed at school. There are convincing arguments on both sides.

2   It's true that cell phones can be very distracting for students. If students are too busy texting, playing games, or checking social media, they aren't as focused on their schoolwork as they should be. They could miss valuable information or not learn something that they will need later on. This can have a negative impact on their grades and on their education.

3   On the other hand, students may need to contact their parents after or even during school. What if an emergency happens? What if the student's after-school activity gets

cancelled and they need a parent to pick them up earlier? What if the parent needs to tell the student that someone else will be picking them up after school? Parents need to be able to get in contact with their children.

4   Students should be able to have their cell phones at school as a safety measure or in case they need to speak to their parents. But they shouldn't be allowed to have their cell phones out during class at all. Students must be responsible enough to have their cell phones at school without letting them distract from the purpose of attending school, which is learning.

1. What is a key detail that is mentioned in both passages?
   A. Students may use cell phones to cheat on assignments or tests.
   B. Students need to be able to contact their parents in case of emergency.
   C. Cell phones can distract students from learning.
   D. Cell phones sometimes go off in class, causing a disruption.

2. On which of the following statements would the author of Passage 1 and the author of Passage 2 disagree?
   A. Students may be distracted by texting and social media.
   B. Students shouldn't have their phones out in class at all.
   C. Cell phones should not be allowed to disrupt learning.
   D. Students should not be allowed to bring phones to school.

3. What is the main difference between Passage 1 and Passage 2? Explain.

_____

_____

_____

_____

_____

_____

4. Which of the following arguments is mentioned in Passage 1, but is not mentioned in Passage 2?
   A. Students may text each other answers or send one another pictures of assignments.
   B. Students could miss important information.
   C. Cell phones are distracting in school.
   D. The purpose of going to school is to learn.

5. List two arguments that are mentioned in Passage 2 but are not mentioned in Passage 1.
   - ☐ Students may need to contact parents in case of an emergency.
   - ☐ Students may be distracted by thinking about checking their cell phones or wondering if someone is texting them.
   - ☐ When students cheat, they don't learn the information for themselves.
   - ☐ Students should be able to have their cell phones at school as a safety measure or in case they need to speak to their parents.

6. The author of Passage 1 mentions that students may use their phones to cheat on assignments or tests. How would the author of Passage 2 most likely respond to this point?
   - **A.** That's why students shouldn't be allowed to have phones at school.
   - **B.** That's not as important as students being able to contact their parents.
   - **C.** This may be true, but students should not be allowed to have their cell phones out in class.
   - **D.** It's unlikely that cell phones would be used in this way.

7. Which passage do you agree with the most? Which arguments convinced you to agree with this passage?

   _____

   _____

   _____

   _____

   _____

   _____

8. Both authors agree that the purpose of school is _____.
   - **A.** Preparing students for adulthood.
   - **B.** Learning.
   - **C.** To understand when you should and should not use your phone during class.
   - **D.** Socializing.

LANGUAGE

DEMONSTRATE COMMAND OF GRAMMAR & USAGE

L.1.1: Demonstrate command of the conventions of standard English grammar and usage when writing or speaking.

1. What is the function of an adjective?
   A. To describe a noun
   B. To tell about an action
   C. To name a person, place, or thing
   D. To take the place of a noun

2. What is the adjective in the sentence below?
   The large dog ran across the street.
   A. street
   B. across
   C. large
   D. dog

3. What is the pronoun in the sentence below?
   Mr. White was scared of dogs, so he ran away.
   A. Mr. White
   B. he
   C. dogs
   D. ran

4. Choose the best adjective to fill in the blank.
   The horse was _____ than the dog.
   A. big
   B. bigger
   C. biggest
   D. more big

5. How would you change the noun bus to make it plural?
   A. Add another -s
   B. Double the -s, then add -es
   C. Add an apostrophe and another -s
   D. Add -es at the end

6. Complete the sentence below with the correct verb.
   I _____ to school yesterday.
   A. walk
   B. walked
   C. walking
   D. will walk

7. Complete the sentence below with the correct verb.
   We will _____ our favorite songs tomorrow in music class.
   A. sing
   B. sang
   C. sung
   D. singing

8. Choose the correct pronoun to agree with the antecedent in the sentence below.
   Michael and Jose both ride _____ bikes to school.

   A. his

   B. our

   C. their

   D. him

9. Complete the sentence below with a coordinating conjunction.
   For my birthday, I want to go to Disney World, _____ I want my best friends to come with me.

   A. but

   B. and

   C. yet

   D. nor

10. Complete the sentence below with a subordinating conjunction.
    _____ school, John always goes to soccer practice.

    A. Although

    B. Whenever

    C. While

    D. After

11. What type of sentence is the sentence below?
    Joey likes to read books, and he also likes to watch movies.

    A. Simple

    B. Compound

    C. Complex

    D. None of the above

12. What type of sentence is the sentence below?
    Jenna also likes to read books, such as chapter books.

    A. Simple

    B. Compound

    C. Complex

    D. None of the above

KNOW CAPITALIZATION, PUNCTUATION & SPELLING

L.1.2 Demonstrate command of the conventions of standard English capitalization, punctuation, and spelling when writing.

1. Which of the following titles is correctly capitalized?
   A. *The Lion, The Witch, And The Wardrobe*
   B. *The Lion, the Witch, And the Wardrobe*
   C. *The Lion, the Witch, and the Wardrobe*
   D. *the Lion, the Witch, and the Wardrobe*

2. Choose the address that uses commas correctly.
   A. 1520 King Street, Orlando, FL, 32825
   B. 1520 King Street Orlando, FL 32825
   C. 1520, King Street, Orlando, FL 32825
   D. 1520 King Street, Orlando, FL 32825

3. Which of the following sentences uses quotation marks and commas correctly?
   A. "I want to go home," said the little girl.
   B. "I want to go home", said the little girl.
   C. "I want to go home, said" the little girl.
   D. "I want to go home, said the little girl."

4. Which of the following sentences uses quotation marks and commas correctly?
   A. "After you finish your vegetables" Mom said, "you can have dessert."
   B. "After you finish your vegetables", Mom said "you can have dessert."
   C. "After you finish your vegetables," Mom said, "you can have dessert."
   D. "After you finish your vegetables Mom said," you can have dessert.

5. Complete the following sentence. The _____ car was shiny and red.
   A. mans
   B. man's
   C. mans'
   D. mans's

6. Complete the following sentence. Students were not allowed in the _____ lounge.
   A. teachers
   B. teacher's
   C. teachers'
   D. teachers's

7. Which of the following sentences is correct?
   A. It always wakes me up when my sister cries.
   B. It always wakes me up when my sister cry's.
   C. It always wakes me up when my sister crys.
   D. It always wakes me up when my sister crie's.

8. What suffix should be added to push to make it past tense?
   Yesterday, I _____ my sister on the swing.
   A. -ness
   B. -ly
   C. -ing
   D. -ed

9. What suffix should be added to sit to make it present tense?
   The class is _____ in the gym until the rain stops.
   A. -ness
   B. -ly
   C. -ing
   D. -ed

10. What suffix should be added to happy to refer to the state of being happy?
    The family was filled with love and _____ when the new baby was born.
    A. -ness
    B. -ly
    C. -ing
    D. -ed

USE APPROPRIATE LANGUAGE CONVENTIONS

L.2.3: Use knowledge of language and its conventions when writing, speaking, reading, or listening.

1. It was finally the big day! Alexis was turning twelve.

   She expected her parents and friends to be as excited about her birthday as she was, but no one mentioned her birthday at breakfast. When Alexis got to school, she was sure her friends would run up to her and say, "Happy birthday". However, no one did.

   After school, Alexis went to soccer practice. She was sad and confused that her birthday had been forgotten. The soccer coach drove Alexis home from practice. Alexis was ready to go to sleep and forget the worst birthday ever. As soon as the coach opened the door, Alexis heard, "HAPPY BIRTHDAY!" and saw balloons, cake, presents, and all of her family and friends. She was definitely _____.

   Choose the word that **best** fills in the blank to describe how Alexis feels at the end of the passage?
   - **A.** sad
   - **B.** confused
   - **C.** upset
   - **D.** surprised

2. Starfish are truly _____ animals. Some of them have five arms, but others have as many as 40. If a starfish ever loses an arm, it can grow it back. Unlike most animals, starfish don't have blood or bones.

   Choose the word that **best** fits in the blank to complete the sentence.
   - **A.** beautiful
   - **B.** unique
   - **C.** boring
   - **D.** common

3. In a village long ago, there lived a massive dragon. He was taller than the tallest castle in the kingdom, and he could breathe fire for miles. Many brave knights had tried to defeat the dragon, but no one could do it. There was a rumor that the dragon was going to destroy the entire village with his fiery breath. All of the villagers were so _____ that they had nightmares for weeks.

Choose the word that best fits in the blank to describe how the villagers feel about the dragon.
   A. excited
   B. terrified
   C. nervous
   D. gloomy

4. Many people believe that Michael Jordan is the greatest basketball player ever. But when he was fifteen-years-old, he tried out for his high school basketball team and didn't make it. After finding out he didn't make the team, Jordan went home, went into his bedroom, and cried.

   Jordan could have given up. He could have decided he would never be a great basketball player. Instead, he used not making the team as _____. It made him work even harder. Whenever he didn't feel like practicing his shot or lifting weights, Jordan closed his eyes. He remembered how he felt when his name wasn't on the team list. That was enough _____ to keep going. The next year, Jordan made the high school basketball team and quickly became their best player.

Choose one word that best fits the blanks to complete the sentences.
   A. motivation
   B. disappointment
   C. happiness
   D. defeat

5. A big scoop of ice cream fell off Melissa's ice cream cone. She felt _____ as she watched her ice cream land on the grass.

Which word best completes the sentence and describes the girl's feelings?
   A. tired
   B. confused
   C. sad
   D. worried

6. What sentence does NOT describe the ocean?

    A. The ocean contains waves, big and small.

    B. I love playing in the ocean.

    C. The ocean is a huge body of salt water.

    D. The ocean is a large area of sea

7. Which sentence best describes a happy puppy?

    A. We could hear him whining from the other room.

    B. He was running faster than the speed of light.

    C. He growled like a lion and showed his teeth.

    D. He jumped around like a bunny rabbit, wagging his tail back and forth.

8. What does this phrase "You crack me up," mean?

    A. You make them laugh.

    B. You broke something.

    C. You hurt them.

    D. You made them cry.

9. What does the phrase "to go the extra mile" mean?"

    A. Walk a long distance.

    B. Keep running after everyone else stops.

    C. Do more than what is expected or required.

    D. Try your best.

10. What does the following sentence mean?

    Miguel stayed home from school because he was feeling a little under the weather.

    A. Miguel stayed home from school because it was too cold.

    B. Miguel stayed home from school because he didn't feel like going anywhere.

    C. Miguel stayed home from school because it might rain.

    D. Miguel stayed home from school because he felt sick.

DETERMINE MEANING OF UNKNOWN WORD/S IN CONTEXT

L.3.4: Determine or clarify the meaning of unknown and multiple-meaning words and phrases based on grade 3 reading and content, choosing flexibly from a range of strategies.

1. Fish, whales, and dolphins are aquatic animals.
   Based on the context clues, what do you think the word **aquatic** means?
   - **A.** Large
   - **B.** Small
   - **C.** Water
   - **D.** Gentle

2. Mom had to **sterilize** the baby's bottle to make sure it was clean.
   What does the word **sterilize** mean in this sentence?
   - **A.** Clean
   - **B.** Buy
   - **C.** Find
   - **D.** Look at

3. Elephants and hippos have a **pewter** color to their skin.
   What does the word **pewter** mean in this sentence? How do the context clues help you?

   _____

   _____

   _____

4. Our waitress was in a bad mood and was not very **cordial** to us.
   What does the word **cordial** mean in this sentence?
   - **A.** Rude
   - **B.** Talkative
   - **C.** Polite
   - **D.** Bored

5. Jimmy was terrible at crossword puzzles, but his sister Julie was very **adept** at them.
   What do you think the word **adept** means in this sentence?
   - **A.** Terrible
   - **B.** Good
   - **C.** Okay
   - **D.** Interested

LANGUAGE

6. The base word **agree** means to have the same opinion about something. What do you think the word **agreeable** means?
    A. Happy
    B. Argumentative
    C. Not able to share the same opinion
    D. Able to share the same opinion

7. The base word **complete** means finished. What does the word **incomplete** mean?

_____

_____

_____

8. What is the difference in meaning between the words **preheat** and **reheat**?

_____

_____

_____

9. What root word do the following words have in common:**Section, bisect, dissect**

_____

_____

    What does the word **bisect** mean?

_____

_____

_____

10. What suffix should be added to happy to refer to the state of being happy?
The family was filled with love and _____ when the new baby was born.
    A. -ness
    B. -ly
    C. -ing
    D. -ed

UNDERSTAND WORD RELATIONSHIPS AND NUANCES IN MEANING

L.3.5: Demonstrate understanding of word relationships and nuances in word meanings.

1. What does the bold phrase mean in the following sentence?
   After Chloe and her best friend Naya had a big argument, Chloe wanted to **take steps** to fix their friendship.
   - **A.** Go for a walk
   - **B.** Take action
   - **C.** Run away
   - **D.** Walk to Naya's house

2. What does the bold phrase mean in the following sentence?
   Max was bigger and stronger than his brother Peter, so Max had the **upper hand** in competitions like wrestling.
   - **A.** The advantage
   - **B.** His hand was on top
   - **C.** His hand was bigger
   - **D.** The disadvantage

3. Is the following sentence figurative or literal? Explain why.
   After practice, Sarah was so hungry she could eat a horse.

   _____

   _____

   _____

4. Is the following sentence figurative or literal? Explain why.
   The boy was as tall as a giraffe.

   _____

   _____

   _____

5. Which word has a similar meaning to **annoyed**?
   - **A.** Amused
   - **B.** Aggravated
   - **C.** Joyful
   - **D.** Confused

6. Which word is similar in meaning to **massive**?

    A. Short

    B. Long

    C. Huge

    D. Tiny

7. Which word means the opposite of **fascinated**?

    A. Scared

    B. Entertained

    C. Happy

    D. Bored

8. Which word could replace the bold word to describe the situation in more detail.

    The boy happily **walked** home.

    A. ran

    B. skipped

    C. stomped

    D. tiptoed

9. Which sentence seems to suggest that Anthony is *most* upset? Explain why.

    A. Anthony was mad.

    B. Anthony was furious.

    C. Anthony was displeased.

    D. Anthony was irritated.

10. Which sentence has a more positive implication?

    A. The girl frowned.

    B. The girl smirked.

    C. The girl laughed.

    D. The girl stared.

11. Find the synonym for the bold word in the sentence below.

    The **sluggish** turtle finished the race last.

    A. Slow

    B. Fast

    C. Speedy

    D. Friendly

KNOW ACADEMIC/DOMAIN-SPECIFIC WORDS

L.3.6: Acquire and use accurately conversational, general academic, and domain specific words and phrases as found in grade appropriate texts, including those that signal spatial and temporal relationships (e.g., After dinner that night we went looking for them).

1. In which of the following classes would you most likely use the word "simile?"
   - **A.** Math
   - **B.** English/Language Arts
   - **C.** Music
   - **D.** Science

2. Which of the following words means "the total amount when adding two or more numbers?"
   - **A.** Perimeter
   - **B.** Area
   - **C.** Sum
   - **D.** Estimate

3. In which class would you most likely learn about "amphibians?"
   - **A.** Math
   - **B.** English/Language Arts
   - **C.** Music
   - **D.** Science

4. What does it mean if your teacher asks you to "use context clues" to figure out the meaning of a word?
   - **A.** Look up the word in the dictionary.
   - **B.** Ask your friend what the word means.
   - **C.** Figure out what the word means based on the information in the sentence.
   - **D.** Raise your hand and ask the teacher for the meaning of the word.

5. In which class would you most likely learn about "antecedents?"
   - **A.** Math
   - **B.** English/Language Arts
   - **C.** Music
   - **D.** Science

6. What does the word "contrast" mean?
    A. Describe similarities between two or more things.
    B. Describe differences between two or more things.
    C. A word that has the same meaning as another word.
    D. List events in order.

7. Choose the most accurate definition of solar system.
    A. The planets and moons that orbit the sun.
    B. The organs and glands in the body that are responsible for digestion.
    C. The process of water circulating between the oceans, atmosphere, and land.
    D. The different types of clouds, including cumulus and cirrus.

8. Select the word or phrase that best completes the sentence below.
    The student who was _____ me in line kept stepping on the back of my shoes.
    A. in front of
    B. behind
    C. next to
    D. to the right of

9. Select the word or phrase that best completes the sentence below.
    We had to wake up early enough to get breakfast _____ school.
    A. in the meantime
    B. during
    C. after
    D. before

10. Select the word or phrase that best completes the sentence below.
    The plane flew far _____ my head.
    A. outside
    B. above
    C. parallel to
    D. in front of

ANSWER EXPLANATIONS

READING LITERATURE

RL.1.1 Ask & Answer Questions Using Text Evidence

1. Part A- **C.** The man believes the cheeses will meet him at the marketplace, which is what he tells them to do when he lets them go.

Part B- **A.** Once the man believes that the cheeses can find their way to the market alone, he states: "Well, then, if you can go to market alone, so can the other cheeses, and I will send them along after you." This statement proves that the man is confident the cheeses will find their way and meet him there.

2. **B.** When the author tell us that the cheeses roll into different bushes, but the man doesn't notice this, we begin to realize that the cheeses will never make their way all the way down to market.

3. After the first cheese escapes, the man says, "So you can run to the market alone, can you? I wish I had known that before. It would have saved me the trouble of carrying you. Well then, if you can go to market alone, so can the other cheeses, and I will send them along after you" (Paragraph 3). As long as students identify any segment of this quote and are able to explain their thinking, the answer should be considered correct. This quote shows that the man is tired of carrying the cheeses and that he believes the first cheese escaped to go to the market. For these reasons, he lets the other cheeses go as well.

4. **B.** Since it is already evening and the cheeses haven't arrived, and since the title of the passage is "The Cheeses That Ran Away," it can be inferred that the man will never find his cheeses. Also, we know that when he rolled the cheeses down the hill, the man didn't realize that some of the cheeses rolled into bushes instead.

5. The man's opinion is that the kettle will follow him home. He gives the kettle directions to where he lives (para 5), and he tells his wife that the kettle is on its way, and "be along in good time." (para 6).

The wife disagrees with the husband and doesn't believe the kettle will arrive at the home. She asks the husband where he left it and "hurries off to get it." The passage also states, "She was not so sure about its coming as he was."

6. In Paragraph 2, the man realizes that the kettle has three legs, while he only has two. This leads him to the decision that the kettle should carry him instead of the other way around.

7. **B.** Both the cheeses and the kettle disobey their owners. The cheeses are told to go to the market and run away instead. The kettle is told to go to the man's home and refuses to walk.

8. Part A- **C.** The woman doesn't think the kettle will come home, which is why she repeatedly asks the man where he has left the kettle.

Part B- **B.** The woman goes to get the kettle and bring it home. After asking her husband where the kettle is located, she "hurries off to get it."

RL.1. 2. Recount Stories & Determine Theme

1. (2) The Grasshopper says there's no need to worry about winter because they have plenty of food at present.

(5) The Grasshopper has no food in the winter and begins to die of starvation, while the ants continue to eat the grain and corn they collected in the summer.

2. Answers may vary. A main lesson is that you should always work hard and prepare for difficult times during the good times. (This is conveyed as the Grasshopper refuses to prepare for the winter and faces the consequences, while the Ant diligently prepares and has plenty of food during the winter.)

3. **D.** We see that the Grasshopper should have prepared like the Ant because the Grasshopper has no food and is starving.

4. The Grasshopper says that there is plenty of food right now, and later he says that winter is still many days away.

5. Answers may vary. One lesson is to listen to your parents. (Icarus is told by his father not to fly too close to the sun, but he ignores the warning and falls into the ocean.)

6. **C.** Icarus doesn't listen to his father. The wax begins to melt, the seagull feathers begin to fall off, and Icarus falls into the ocean and drowns. This teaches the lesson that Icarus should have listened to his father, and children should listen to their parents.

7. **B.** The beginning of the passage states that the father of Icarus and Icarus are imprisoned because the father is a very talented inventor, and the King wants Icarus' father to only make inventions for him.

8. **D.** Only the title "The Disobedient Son" does a good job of summarizing the story and conveying its overall message. "Flying," "The Inventor and his Inventions," and "The Greedy King" are too

specific and not representative of the story as a whole.

RL.1.3 Describe Characters & Explain Their Actions

1. **B.** They both have positive attitudes. Each time a problem happens during the camp out, Jessica and Tia do their best to stay positive and still enjoy themselves.

2. **A.** She's a good friend. The passage also says that Tia didn't want Jessica to feel bad about forgetting the marshmallows, which shows she cares about her friend's feelings.

3. Answers may vary. Students should say that they would or would not like to be friends with Tia and Jessica, and they should provide at least one detail from the passage to support their response. For example, students might say that they would like to be friends with the girls because they seem nice (like when Tia didn't want Jessica to feel bad) and try to make the best of any situation (like when they try to enjoy the smores even though they aren't the same).

4. **2nd and 4th Choice.** Both of these details show the girls being flexible by adapting to the problems that occur on the camp out.

5. At the beginning, Lauren doesn't like raking leaves. (She pouts and sighs while dragging the rake "for what felt like the hundredth time.") After spending the day raking leaves with Drew, Lauren learns to enjoy raking. (She smiles when her dad says raking leaves should be her chore from now on and says, "Raking leaves isn't so bad."). There are other details that could be added, but these are some of the main ones.

6. Part A- **A.** Like Tia and Jessica in the first passage, Drew can make the best of a bad situation. He makes raking leaves fun by playing games and having a positive attitude about raking.

Part B- **C.** Drew responds enthusiastically when Lauren asks if he's sure about helping with the leaves, and he immediately suggests a way to make raking more fun.

7. Drew is a good friend because he volunteers to help Lauren with raking the leaves, and he tries to cheer her up and make her task more fun with games like leaf jumping and races.

8. Lauren: She doesn't like raking leaves.

Supporting Detail: She sighs and pouts while raking the leaves, and she can't believe that anyone would volunteer to help with something so boring.

Drew: He doesn't mind raking leaves.

Supporting Detail: He volunteers to help Lauren. When she asks if he's sure, he enthusiastically says, "Of course!" Immediately, he begins finding ways to make raking the leaves more fun.

RL.2.4 Determine Word Meaning In Context

1. **A.** The author is nervous. The text says that the author is worried, and it also says that the author has practiced for weeks. We know that she's prepared, but she's still nervous that something might go wrong.

2. Fell asleep. Readers can guess that "dozed off" means fell asleep because the text says that Josie was bored and tired.

3. The phrases "straight down" and "into the water" tell readers that plunge means to fall down. The fact that the bridge is old and Peter must walk carefully are additional hints.

4. The author compares his struggles in math class to climbing a mountain. He says, "We all have challenges in life. We all have our mountains to climb. For me, it's math class." He also talks about working hard and eventually "reaching the top."

5. **A.** Fast. Liz wins every race, and it's never even close. This tells us that Liz is very fast.

6. **C.** Courage. Peter is the only one who is brave enough to go into Old Man Frank's yard; everyone else is too scared.

7. **B.** "…and listened for the sound of Old Man Frank yelling." The fact that they are listening for a noise shows readers that "caught our breath" means to be silent and wait.

8. Answers may vary. There are several clues: the phrase, "Except he wasn't yelling" shows that the boys were wrong in their assumptions (guesses) about Old Man Frank. The sentence, "It seemed like he wasn't so scary after all," also indicates that the boys had guessed incorrectly. Details like Old Man Frank asking friendly questions and telling stories about his childhood provide additional clues.

RL.2.5 Identify & Understand Parts Of Texts

1. **B.** A poem. Poems are divided into stanzas like stories are divided into paragraphs.

2. **B.** Scene. Plays are divided into scenes like stories are divided into paragraphs.

3. **C.** Line breaks are used to enhance ideas and

meaning in a poem.

4. At the beginning of the story, so readers understand where the story takes place and who the characters are. It would be confusing if setting and characters were introduced later in the story.

5. At the end, because the story is over once the problem is solved. There's no reason to continue the story when there's no problem to solve.

6. **B.** There are four stanzas in this poem

7. **C.** The little master should appreciate that the sheep grows wool that will be used to make the master's clothing.

8. **B.** These lines show that when spring is over, the sheep's wool is cut to warm the master through the cold winter. While the sheep may seem lazy in the spring, he benefits the master in the winter.

RL.2.6 Identify Point Of View of Self & Author/Characters

1. **C.** Point of view is who is narrating or telling the story. It's the perspective from which the story is told.

2. **B.** Third-person point of view is when a character is not an active participant in the story. Words like "he," "she," and "they" are used.

3. Part A- **C.** A puppy is the narrator of the story.

Part B- **B.** The man who brings the puppy home. It isn't clear that the narrator is a puppy until the man says, "Hi, little puppy!"

4. **A.** The story is told from the first-person point of view. The narrator, the puppy, is an active participant in the story, and he uses words like "I."

5. The author makes the reader feel sad and worried for the puppy. Details like the puppy being cold, people honking and yelling at the puppy, and the puppy being hungry create this feeling.

6. **C.** The puppy is cold because of the rain, and he's trying to find shelter.

7. Part A- **B** "...but she didn't look very happy." This quote shows that the woman will allow the puppy to stay at her house, but she doesn't truly want him to be there.

Part B- **A.** The woman doesn't know that the dog is homeless. This might make her feel more sorry for the puppy and want to help him.

8. All of the other human characters in the story don't like the dog and don't want to help him. People honk at the puppy, and someone yells, "Get out of the way!" Another man tells the puppy, "Get lost!" Susie, the man's wife, says, "Are you crazy?" when the man brings the puppy home. Only the man is nice to the puppy, calling him cute, asking if he has anywhere to go, and bringing him home.

RL.3.7 Identify How Illustrations Convey Information

1. Answers may vary. Nathan and Julie got off the school bus, and they're excited about having a great first day of school.

2. Answers may vary. Nathan and Julie seem like they feel happy in this picture. The twins are smiling. They are walking with big strides, or possibly skipping. The text says that they're finally in the same class, their new teacher seems nice, and most of their best friends are in the class too. It also says that they're confident third grade will be a good year.

3. Some of the clues that the author gives that prove Nathan and Julie feel like they will have a great year in third grade is: they've never been in the same class before, but they are this year; their new teacher seems very nice, and many of their best friends are also in their class. In the pictures, both Nathan and Julie are smiling, they're holding hands, and they're walking with big strides or skipping. This shows they are confident about having a great third grade year.

4. **B.** In comparison to the person in the photo, this image emphasizes the dog's massive size (which is described in the text).

5. **D.** As the text also explains, this image shows that the dog is sweet and loving. His hands are on the girl's shoulders, almost like a hug. It looks like he's being very gentle despite his size.

6. The purpose of this image is to help readers visualize the information in the text (or to further emphasize the information in the text). In the text, the writer explains that although her dog is huge, he's very sweet and loving. The image shows that the dog is enormous as well, but it also shows that the dog is loving and gentle. He's not mean or scary, as some people assume based on his size.

7. Answers may vary. The boy looks as though he's feeling scared or nervous. Evidence that the boy looks scared or nervous is that his eyes are wide, his mouth is curved and his teeth are

showing, his hands are up to defend himself, the bee is looking at him angrily, and it looks as though several more bees are coming out of the beehive.

RL. 3.9 Compare & Contrast Narratives

1. Both the farmer and the dog are greedy and want more than they already have. The farmer wants more than one golden egg each day, and the dog wants a bigger bone. They both attempt to gain more and instead lose what they already had (the goose for the farmer and the bone for the dog).

2. Part A- **B.** The golden goose and the farmer live on a farm.

Part B- **A.** The dog is walking past a river when he thinks his reflection is another dog with a bigger bone.

3. Part A- **D.** Both characters should have been grateful for what they have instead of being greedy. Then the farmer would still have his golden goose and the dog would still have his bone. Instead, both characters end up with nothing.

Part B- **D.** The fact that the farmer's goose dies at the end of the story develops the theme that the farmer should have been grateful for what he had instead of being greedy.

4. The farmer's decision: To cut open the goose for more eggs

The result: There are no eggs inside the goose, and the goose dies.

The dog's decision: To jump into the river in an attempt to get a bigger bone from the "other dog" (which was really his reflection).

The result: The dog has to frantically swim to shore, loses his bone, and of course does not get a bigger bone either.

5. **A.** In both stories, the conflict occurs as the result of the main characters not being satisfied with what they have.

6. The farmer cut open his goose in hopes of getting more golden eggs. The story explains that the goose only laid one golden egg each day, and the farmer was getting impatient. He wanted more eggs and more money, so he decided to cut open the goose.

7. The dog jumped into the river because he thought his reflection was another dog with a bigger bone than the one he had been given by the butcher. The passage explains that if the dog had thought for a moment, he might have realized his mistake. Instead, he impulsively jumped into the river to try to get the bigger bone from the dog.

8. All options show the farmer and dog are different except the 4th and the 6th option, which contain information that is either incorrect or not in the passage.

READING INFORMATION

RI.1.1 Ask & Answer Questions Using Text Evidence

1. **B.** The starfish is not a fish. The passage explains that scientists are trying to change the name to "sea star" since starfish are not actually fish.

2. **C.** The passage mentions that starfish use their colors as camouflage and to scare off predators and that starfish have hard, bony skin that can protect them from predators. However, starfish don't have sharp spikes on their arms.

3. Answers may vary. Some possible answers are:
1) The starfish doesn't have blood or brains.

2) The starfish can regrow its arms and even grow a whole new starfish from its arm.

3) Starfish have one eye on the tip of each arm and can't see color.

4. The text says that many starfish have 5 arms, but some species of starfish have 10, 20, or even 40 arms.

5. **(2)** The virus makes the starfish weak.

(4) The starfish develops white sores on its body.

(5) The arms sometimes rip off and walk away.

6. **A.** The beginning of the passage states that starfish were dying out "across North America."

7. Part A- **B.** The virus normally affects just one or two species, but now over 20 species have been affected.

Part B- **C.** Scientists think the virus may be spreading more quickly because there are so many starfish packed into small areas.

8. The passage says scientists will continue to study the parvovirus. They want to stop the virus, but if they can't do that, they want to learn more about the virus so they can prevent an outbreak like this one in the future.

RI.1.2 Determine Main Idea & Explain Key Details

1. **B.** The main idea of this passage is that potato chips were an accidental invention. The passage goes on to provide details of exactly how potato

chips were accidentally invented.

2. Answers may vary. Possibilities include, "George Crum's customers complained that his fried potatoes were too thick and bland, so he tried to make disgusting fried potatoes that were too thin and too salty," or, "Instead, the customers loved the fried potatoes, and soon everyone was talking about the tasty new invention of potato chips." Students may also cite the first or last lines of the text, which specifically mention that potato chips were an accidental invention.

3. **C.** This sentence supports the idea that potato chips were not intentionally invented. Instead, they originated from a hotel chef trying to prank some customers who didn't like his food.

4. **D.** The title "Potato Chips: A Happy Accident" represents the main idea of this passage well. The other three choices focus on specific details or aspects of the text that don't represent the text as a whole.

5. **A.** This passage focuses on the idea that although people long believed that Abner Doubleday invented baseball, we don't know who truly invented the sport.

6. Answers may vary. Possibilities include, "Until 2011, popular legend was that a man named Abner Doubleday invented baseball," and, "The rumor was so popular that the Baseball Hall of Fame was opened in Cooperstown, New York, where baseball was supposedly invented." These statements support the idea that the legend of Abner Doubleday was very popular. The following details support the idea that Doubleday didn't invent baseball, and we don't know who did: Historian John Thorn published a book explaining that baseball was played long before 1839, various versions of the game existed in New York, Philadelphia, Massachusetts, and Britain, and John Thorn says the question of who invented baseball is one we may never be able to answer.

7. **D.** The information about Abner Doubleday being a Civil War general does not support or relate to the main idea of the passage (the invention of baseball).

8. **C.** The passage explains that we'll probably never know who invented baseball (mostly because some many variations of it were played in many different locations).

RI.1.3 Describe & Understand Relationships Between Ideas

1. **B.** People believed that the *Titanic* was unsinkable and that nothing bad could happen to the ship, so they didn't have as many lifeboats as they

should have.

2. **A.** The passage explains that many historians think the captain of the ship was trying to beat the time of another ship, the *Olympic*.

3. Students should include any two possible details: People believed that the *Titanic* was "the safest ship ever" and it was unsinkable, warnings about icebergs were ignored, the captain was traveling too fast in an effort to beat the time of another ship, and there were only enough lifeboats for half the passengers and crew.

4. Because people believed the *Titanic* was so safe, they made poor decisions. They believed that nothing bad could happen to the ship, so there weren't enough lifeboats on board for everyone. If they hadn't believed that the ship was unsinkable, they might have taken the warnings about icebergs more seriously. The captain might have also traveled more slowly and safely. As a result, damages to the ship and the loss of passengers and crew was much worse than it might have been if people had been more cautious.

5. The entire city was constructed of wood, firefighters were exhausted because of the 20 fires that had occurred the previous week, and firefighters were sent to the wrong neighborhood at first.

6. **C.** The firefighters were sent to the wrong neighborhood at first, so the fire was out of control by the time they finally arrived at the O'Leary home.

7. **B.** The people of Chicago blamed Mrs. O'Leary and her cow. The passage explains that even though Mrs. O'Leary told reporters she was sleeping when the fire started, the newspapers reported that she was milking the cow and the cow kicked over a lantern, starting the destructive fire.

8. When the city was reconstructed, architects built some of the first skyscrapers. The population and economy grew, and the city of Chicago became a great city.

9. Mrs. O'Leary barely left her house after the Chicago Fire. She avoided other people because almost the entire city blamed her for the fire and felt angry about the destruction she had supposedly caused.

10. **B.** The fire finally stopped two days later when it rained.

11. Both passages are about accidents or disasters that are thought to have happened because of a person's actions. The *Titanic* passage reveals that historians believe that the captain of the *Titanic* made the ship go too fast for icy waters, which resulted in the crash. In the Great Chicago Fire passage, the newspapers reported that Ms O'Leary knocked over a lamp which started the fire. Also, in both passages, some people lost their lives because the thing/person(s) expected to save them did not. In the case of the *Titanic,* there were not enough lifeboats on the ship to get all the people to safety. In the Great Chicago Fire, the firefighters were not able to put the fire out (the rain eventually put the fire out), and hundreds of people died.

RI.2.4 Determine Domain-Specific Word Meaning in Context

1. **A.** We know that prevalent means "common" because the next sentence mentions that people visit from all over to see the "many" cacti in these states.

2. A succulent is a plant that can store water. The passage explains that cacti can store water in their stems, roots, and leaves and can survive without rain for up to a year.

3. **B.** Hue means color. This part of the passage is about how most cacti are green, but some are slightly different colors like brownish and bluish.

4. **D.** Imagine. The sentence suggests that "picture" is a synonym for "envision," so readers can infer that "imagine" is a synonym as well.

5. A chocolatier is a person who makes chocolate. The passage states, "To transform these bitter cocoa beans into delicious chocolate, chocolatiers have to first dry out the beans." This suggests that the chocolatier is the person who takes the cocoa beans and makes them into chocolate.

6. **C.** In this sentence, "the finished product" refers to the chocolate. The cocoa beans and cocoa nibs occur earlier in the process. The very next sentence starts with the words, "The chocolate," which shows us that the author used the phrase "the finished product" to refer to the

chocolate. Later, a candy bar is introduced as one treat that can be made with the chocolate.

7. **B.** The cocoa liquor and cocoa butter are removed from the cocoa nibs.

8. **A** and **C.** The chocolate bar travels from one place to another to get to the consumer, and it also undergoes a long process as it is transformed from cocoa beans into chocolate. "A fun trip or vacation" or 'ocean voyage' doesn't make sense in this context, and although "hard work" is required to make the chocolate, it's NOT a definition for the word "journey."

RI.2.5 Use Text Features & Search Tools

1. **C.** Headings are intended to help readers find the main idea of sections in order to locate information easily.

2. **B.** Bold text is used to indicate key words and phrases and draw the reader's attention to this essential information.

3. **D.** This section contains information about rock features, including stalactites, which are rock formations that hang from the ceiling.

4. **B.** Bats are cave creatures, which are discussed under the heading "Cave Creatures."

5. **A.** Paragraphs. The key difference between solutional caves and sea caves is provided in paragraphs (Paragraphs 4 and 5), including the facts that, solutional caves are formed by rainfall and chemical processes, while sea caves are formed by erosion.

6. Part A- **D.** The article explains that sea caves form when sea cliffs are eroded by waves and tides.

Part B- **B** and **C.** Readers could immediately go to the heading "Types of Caves" to find information about sea caves. They could then quickly locate the definition using the bolded text.

7. **D.** Searching "Cave types" would lead to information about all the different kinds of caves. Searching "Solutional caves" would only provide information on one type of cave rather than on many different types.

8. **A.** A glossary is an alphabetical list of words with definitions. An index is a listing of the

contents of a book or article by page number.

RI.2.6 Identify Point Of View of Self & Author

1. **1st and 3rd Choices.** These sentences best express the author's overall point of view: that exercise offers many excellent benefits. The other two options are specific details that support this viewpoint.

2. Part A - **C.** The author might agree with options A and B, but we don't know this information based on the text. D is incorrect because the author points out that you don't have to go to the gym to experience the benefits of exercise.

Part B- **D.** This piece of evidence includes information about exercise benefitting both the body and the mind.

3. Answers will vary. Correct answers will include an explanation of why students agree or disagree with the viewpoint stated in the article (that exercising is beneficial and important). They will state specific details from the passage and explain how they influenced the student's point of view (to agree or disagree with the author's viewpoint) Example:" I agree with the viewpoint that exercise is important for your body and mind. When you exercise, you can maintain a healthy body weight and at the same time, you will feel happier and more relaxed. It also helps prevent diseases that harm your health, like diabetes." The passage contains less evidence to use if a student disagrees with the author.

4. **C.** The author's point of view is that too much TV is harmful. The other details are included in the article, but they're too specific and don't represent the author's overall viewpoint.

5. **A.** "Don't overdo it," best summarizes the author's point of view about television. The other words don't give us enough information to express the author's viewpoint.

6. Part A- **C.** A is incorrect because the author believes TV is fine in moderation. B is never mentioned in the passage. D is too much of a generalization. The author does say that kids who witness bad behaviors on TV may imitate it, but does not claim that all kids who watch TV behave badly.

Part B- **B.** This quote shows that the author believes activities like reading and spending time with family are healthier than watching television.

7. Answers may vary. Correct answers will state whether the student agrees or disagrees with the author's viewpoint (that too much television harms children) and explain the reasoning behind this stance. Student reasoning for whether they agree or disagree must be supported with information from the passage. For this reason, it makes it difficult for students to disagree with the author's viewpoint. The passage is filled with facts supporting why children need to watch less television. A typical child will likely disagree with the article because they like to watch television or because they disagree that watching television is unhealthy or can lead to violent behavior. However, these are opinions based on the student's thinking and not based on the facts from the article.

8. The title of the article is "Turn Off the TV." Immediately, readers understand that the author may think television (or too much television) is bad, since the author is encouraging people to stop watching.

RI.3.7 Use & Understand Information In Illustrations

1. **A.** The passage explains that gas molecules are spread out, and the image also shows that they are by far the most spread out molecules among the states of matter.

2. **C.** The illustration helps readers visualize the information that is provided in the text, and, in this case, also adds new information (with the arrows and labels) about the ways that states of matter change.

3. **C.** The shape of a solid does not change, even if it's placed in a container.

4. Liquid, Solid. The arrow and "Freezing" label on the image indicates that a liquid can change into a solid through the process of freezing.

5. Based on the illustration, it looks like a liquid can turn into a gas. There are arrows

pointing from the liquid to the gas with the label "evaporation".

6. **1st and 3rd Choices.** Gas and liquid molecules move around, but solid molecules don't. Condensation is not a type of molecule.

7. **B.** Europa is the only one of Jupiter's four largest moons that is not larger than Earth's moon.

8. **D.** Saturn's moon Titan is much larger than Earth's moon. Neptune's moon Triton looks close in size to Earth's moon, but Titan is much bigger, making Saturn the better answer.

RI.3.8 Describe & Make Connections In Text

1. **B.** The information in Paragraph 2 introduces the reader to Bethany's passion for surfing. The author states that "Bethany was home schooled so that she could pursue her passion for surfing." It also describes how Bethany is able to beat people who have surfed longer than her, so we can infer that she works hard and really enjoys surfing.

2. **B.** Paragraph 3 introduces the cause which is Bethany is attacked by the shark. Paragraph 4 introduces the effects of shark attack such as: she has to go to the hospital, she loses a lot of blood, she loses her arm, and she has to have a lot of surgeries.

3. Paragraph 5 shows us that Bethany did not stop surfing just because she lost her arm. It also shows us that Bethany refused to give up. Students may include any of the following details to support their answer: "Despite losing her arm, Bethany pledged to get back to surfing as soon as possible." Also, just one month after the attack, Bethany returned to surfing. Lastly, she continued to be a great surfer with one arm because she won awards and competitions.

4. **2nd, 3rd, 5th & 6th Choices.** Students should select the following answer choices: Bethany undergoes many surgeries, Bethany loses her arm, Bethany loses a lot of blood, and Bethany makes a promise to herself to return to surfing. The 4th answer choice, Bethany has to stay in the hospital for several months, is incorrect because the passage states that

Bethany is released from the hospital a few days later.

5. **D.** In Paragraph 3, we learn that school is very hard for Patricia. We learn that she tried to learn how to read and write, but she just couldn't do it. There are no clues in this paragraph that Patricia is a bad student or that she could have tried harder. It is not interesting background information about Patricia because it is important for the reader to understand that Patricia still couldn't read or write, despite trying very hard in school.

6. **A.** In Paragraph 1, we are introduced to Patricia and her family. In Paragraph 2, we learn more about Patricia and her family. We learn that her parents got divorced, and we learn that Patricia has to live in two separate places. There is no cause/effect or problem/solution relationship between Paragraph 1 and Paragraph 2.

7. Answers may vary. Several factors have helped Patricia to become a famous author. In Paragraph 5, we learn that she is diagnosed with dyslexia and finally gets the help she needs. Therefore, Patricia learns how to read. In Paragraph 6, the author explains that Patricia is a wonderful example of what can happen if we work hard and never give up. Students may also include that Patricia still went to school and worked hard even though she was bullied. Students should include any 2 of these reasons.

8. **B.** Paragraph 4 gives us some insight into the bullying that Patricia encountered. As a result, we know that she started to hate school because the author states: "Eventually, she despised going to school." While students may be tempted to selected Letter D, the focus of this paragraph is not to describe why bullying is bad. Furthermore, the paragraph does not describe the full effects that bullying has on Patricia other than she despised going to school.

RI.3.9. Compare And Contrast Key Points In Two Texts

1. **C.** Both passages acknowledge that cell phones may distract students from learning.

2. **D.** The author of Passage 1 thinks that students shouldn't be allowed to have phones

at school at all, while the author of Passage 2 thinks students should be able to have phones at school and simply not allowed to take them out in class.

3. The author of Passage 1 thinks cell phones shouldn't be allowed in school at all, and Passage 1 only addresses bad aspects of cell phone usage. Passage 2 addresses both sides of the issue and explain some reasons that cell phones may be good to have at school.

4. **A.** Passage 1 mentions that students may use cell phones to share answers on assignments and tests. The rest of the answer choices are mentioned in both passages, although they may not be stated in the exact words as the answer choices.

5. **1st & 4th answer choices**: (1): Students may need to contact parents in case of emergency.(4) Students and parents may need to contact one another if plans related to transportation or pick up times change.

6. **C.** The author of Passage 2 would likely say that rules about students not having cell phones in class must be enforced, or that students must be responsible enough not to use cell phones in class. However, she would argue that students do need to have cell phones at school for safety reasons and to be able to contact parents as needed (and vice versa).

7. Responses may vary. Correct answers will take a position for Passage 1 or for Passage 2 and will mention key arguments from the passage that the student found convincing.

An example of a student explanation who agrees with Passage 1 may state: I agree with Passage 1 the most. I agree with Passage 1 because cell phones do cause too much temptation. If you are too busy looking at your phone or even thinking about your phone, you are missing important information from the teacher.

An example of a student explanation who agrees with Passage 2 may state: I agree with Passage 2 the most. I agree with Passage 2 because I think students need to have them in case of an emergency. Students should be responsible enough to keep their cell phones in their backpacks during school time so that they do not get distracted.

8. **B.** Learning. Both passages mention that school is about learning and that cell phones should not interrupt the learning process.

LANGUAGE

L.1.1 Demonstrate Command of Grammar & Usage

1. **A.** Adjectives are used to describe or clarify nouns by giving more information about their size, color, shape, age, material, etc.

2. **C.** The word *large* describes the noun dog, giving readers more information about its size.

3. **B.** The word *he* is a pronoun used to replace the antecedent *Mr. White.*

4. **B.** The comparative adjective *bigger* correctly completes this sentence, which compares the size of the horse to the size of the dog. -Er is added to the end of adjectives when they adjective is used to compare two nouns.

5. **D.** The plural form of the noun *bus* is the plural noun buses, so we must add an -es to the end of the word.

6. **B.** *Walked* agrees with the first-person subject I and the tense (past). This sentence is in past tense because of the word *yesterday.*

7. **A.** *Sing* correctly completes this sentence. *Sang* and *sung* are past tense, while *singing* is present tense. When combined with *will, sing* is future tense and agrees with the first-person plural subject *we.*

8. **C.** *Their* agrees with the antecedent *Michael and Jose.*

9. **B.** The speaker of the sentence wants to both go to Disney World and bring her best friends, requiring the coordinating conjunction *and.* The two sentences do not contrast, so we can't use *but* or *yet,* and *nor* is used for negative possibilities.

10. **D.** It makes sense for John to go to soccer practice *after* school. Additionally, none of the other possible options form grammatically correct sentences.

11. **B.** This sentence contains two independent clauses, so it is compound. An independent clause is a clause that can stand by itself as a sentence.

12. **C.** This sentence is complex because it contains both a dependent clause and an independent clause. A dependent clause is a clause that cannot stand by itself as a sentence.

L.1.2 Know Capitalization, Punctuation & Spelling

1. **C.** In titles, it is necessary to capitalize the first and last word, in addition to nouns, pronouns, verbs, and adjectives. In this title, *Lion, Witch,* and *Wardrobe* need to be capitalized. *The* must also be capitalized because it is the first word in the sentence, but any additional appearance of *the* must be lowercase. The word *and* is not capitalized because it is a conjunction.

2. **D.** When an address is written as a line of text, commas must separate the street, state, and city. Commas are not needed between words and numbers, such as the building number or the zip code.

3. **A.** Quotation marks must go only around dialogue, and the comma should be placed before the closing quotation marks.

4. **C.** This sentence correctly puts quotation marks only around dialogue. There is a comma before the closing quotation marks and between the word *said* and the additional dialogue.

5. **B.** The apostrophe s indicates possession, showing that the car belongs to the man.

6. **C.** With a plural noun, like teachers, the possessive apostrophe comes after the s instead of before. This is to indicate that the noun is both plural and possessive.

7. **A.** *Cries* is the correct spelling for the present tense form of *cry*. Cry ends with a *-y* so the *-y* is replaced by an *-i* before adding the *-es* ending.

8. **D.** The suffix -ed indicates that a verb is past tense.

9. **C.** The suffix -ing indicates that a verb is present tense.

10. **A.** The suffix -ness means "the state of" something. In this case, *happiness* is the correct word to refer to the state of being happy.

L.2.3 Use Appropriate Language Conventions

1. **D.** Alexis was sad throughout the day because she thought everyone forgot her birthday. Before Alexis goes into the house, she thinks about how she wants to go to sleep and forget "the worst birthday ever." Based on this information, readers know that Alexis was surprised when she saw all of her friends, family, cake, and presents.

2. **B.** The characteristics listed are not common, making the starfish unique. Additionally, the phrase "unlike most animals" also hints that the correct answer is "unique."

3. **B.** The fact that the villagers had nightmares for weeks indicates that they feel terrified. *Nervous* is not strong enough to describe the way people would feel about a giant fire-breathing dragon.

4. **A.** The first blank is contrasted with what Michael Jordan could have done after not making the team (given up and decided he would never be a great basketball player). This suggests that he used not making the team as motivation. The second blank indicates that the correct word is something that can keep a person going, also showing that motivation is the correct answer.

5. **C.** The girl would feel sad about her ice cream falling on the ground. The usage of "fell" also shows that this was an accident that was not meant to happen, so readers can infer the girl felt sad about it.

6. **B.** This sentence is not a good description of the ocean. Choices A, C and D offer facts about the ocean. Choice B states an opinion that is relevant to one person.

7. **D.** This answer choice best describes a happy puppy. Choices A and C describe behaviors we would more likely see from a sad or angry puppy. Choice B doesn't necessarily indicate that the puppy is happy, so it's not a good description.

8. **A.** "You crack me up," means that someone is funny and makes you laugh.

9. **C.** Going the extra mile has nothing to do with physical distances or running. It simply means going above and beyond what is expected or required.

10. **D.** Being "under the weather" means being sick. It's also the most logical answer choice listed.

L.3.4 Determine Meaning of Unknown Word/s in Context

1. **C.** Based on the examples of *fish, whales,* and *dolphins,* we can determine that the word **aquatic** is related to water. From the answer choices provided, water is the only option that all three examples have in common.

2. **A.** The definition of the word **sterilize** appears in the sentence when it's explained that the reason Mom sterilized the bottle was to "make sure it was clean."

3. An example of a student explanation: **Pewter** means gray. Both elephants and hippos have gray skin. The word *color* is another context clue in this sentence.

4. **C.** Because the waitress was in a bad mood, we can infer that she was not very polite to the customers.

5. **B.** This sentence indicates that the word **adept** must contrast with the word *terrible.* We know this because Jimmy was terrible at crossword puzzles, *but* his sister was very adept at them.

6. **D.** If agree means to share the same opinion about something, agreeable must mean that people are capable of/able to share an opinion on a topic.

7. Incomplete means not finished. The prefix *in* means *in, on,* or *not.* In this context, the only definition that makes sense is "not complete."

8. Preheat means to heat before, while reheat means to heat again. The prefix *pre* means *prior to, before, in advance of,* or *early,* and the prefix *re* means *back* or *again.*

9. Each of these words share the root word **sect.** The root word **sect** means cut. The prefix **bi** means twice or two. **Bisect** means to cut in two.

10. **A.** To use the word *happy* as a noun, the state of being happy, you need to use the suffix -ness. The suffix -ly transforms *happy* into an adverb. The suffixes -ing and -ed cannot be used because they would not transform *happy* into real words.

L.3.5 Understand Word Relationships and Nuances in Meaning

1. **B.** In this sentence, the phrase *take steps* is used figuratively to mean take action or do something about it. Literal walking or running probably won't fix Chloe's relationship with her friend Naya, but taking action will.

2. **A.** This is another example of figurative language. When the sentence says that Max has *the upper hand,* it means he has the advantage over his brother. His hand being on top or being bigger is not relevant to the context of the sentence, which describes a wrestling competition. We can infer that Max has the advantage, and not the disadvantage, because he is bigger and stronger than his brother.

3. The sentence is figurative. Sarah could not literally eat a horse (and probably wouldn't want to either). This is hyperbole (exaggerated for effect), and meant to express that Sarah is extremely hungry. An example of an appropriate student explanation may state: This sentence is figurative. I know this because Sarah could not actually eat a horse. The phrase *could eat a horse* is used to show that someone is very hungry.

4. The sentence is figurative. The boy is not literally as tall as a giraffe. This is a simile meant to express that the boy is very tall. An example of an appropriate student explanation may state: This sentence is figurative. I know this because it is not possible for the boy to actually be as tall as a giraffe. The phrase as tall *as a giraffe* is used to show that someone is incredibly tall.

5. **B.** *Aggravated* is similar in meaning to *annoyed. Amused* and *joyful* are both positive words, while *annoyed* is negative. *Confused* is not relevant or close in meaning to *annoyed.*

6. **C.** *Massive* means large, so *huge* is similar in meaning. It does not refer specifically to height or length, so *short* and *long* are incorrect. *Tiny* is an antonym for *massive,* not a synonym.

7. **D.** *Fascinated* means interested or awestruck,

so *bored* has the opposite meaning. *Entertained* is very close in meaning to *fascinated,* while *happy* and *scared* aren't related.

8. **B.** The word *skipped* implies that the boy was happy on his walk home, as mentioned in the sentence. *Stomped* has an angry connotation, while there's nothing in the sentence to suggest that *ran* or *tiptoed* would be a more accurate description.

9. **B.** *Furious* is a much stronger word than *mad, displeased* or *irritated.* Choice B is more powerful and implies that Anthony is more upset. An example of an appropriate student explanation may state: Furious shows that Anthony is the most upset. I know this because the words *mad, displeased,* and *irritated* do not show that Anthony is very upset.

10. **C.** Laughing is the only positive word among these choices. Frowning and smirking all have somewhat negative connotations. Staring is not related.

11. **A.** If students don't know the meaning of the word *sluggish,* it can still be inferred that *slow* is a synonym, since the turtle finished the race last. *Speedy* and *fast* wouldn't make sense in this context, and *friendly* is irrelevant to the sentence.

L.3.6 Know Academic/ Domain-Specific Words

1. **B.** A simile is a type of figurative language that students would learn about in English/ Language Arts class.

2. **C.** The total amount when adding two or more numbers is a sum.

3. **D.** Amphibians are a class of animal that students would learn about in Science.

4. **C.** Using context clues means using the known words and phrases in a sentence to determine the meaning of the unknown word.

5. **B.** Antecedents are the nouns replaced by pronouns, and students would learn this term in English/Language Arts class.

6. **B.** Contrast means to describe the differences between two or more items.

7. **A.** The Solar System refers to the planets and moons that orbit the sun. Choice B describes the digestive system, Choice C describes the water cycle, and Choice D describes cloud types.

8. **B.** The phrase "stepping on the back of my shoes" indicates that the student is behind the writer. Additionally, the fact that the students are in line indicates "to the right of" and "next to" are most likely incorrect answers.

9. **D.** We can infer that the correct answer is "before" because the sentence includes the phrase "wake up early enough."

10. **B.** The use of the phrase "my head," in addition to knowledge about the location of an airplane, indicates that the correct answer is "above."

ANSWER EXPLANATIONS

PRACTICE TESTS

ELA
Practice Test One

Session One
(Reading)

Directions: Read the passage "My Father Meets the Cat" and then answer Numbers 1 through 8.

Passage 1: "My Father Meets the Cat," an excerpt from My Father's Dragon
by Ruth Stiles Gannett

1   One cold rainy day when my father was a little boy, he met an old alley cat on his street. The cat was very drippy and uncomfortable so my father said, "Wouldn't you like to come home with me?"

2   This surprised the cat—she had never before met anyone who cared about old alley cats—but she said, "I'd be very much obliged if I could sit by a warm furnace, and perhaps have a saucer of milk."

3   My father and the cat became good friends. One day, my father and the cat went for a walk in the park.

4   My father said, "When I grow up I'm going to have an airplane. Wouldn't it be wonderful to fly just anywhere you might think of!"

5   "Would you like to fly very, very much?" asked the cat.

6   "I certainly would. I'd do anything if I could fly."

7   "Well," said the cat, "If you'd really like to fly that much, I think I know of a sort of a way you might get to fly while you're still a little boy."

8   "You mean you know where I could get an airplane?"

9   "Well, not exactly an airplane, but something even better..."

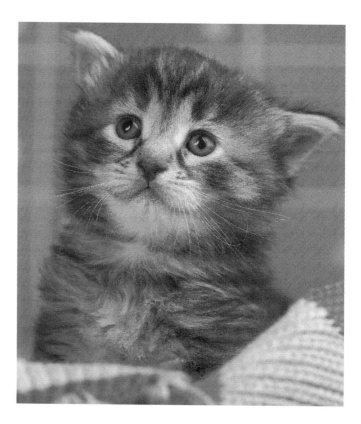

Now answer Numbers 1 through 8. Base your answers on the passage "My Father Meets the Cat," an excerpt from **My Father's Dragon.**

1. Who is the narrator of this story?
   (A) A son or daughter
   (B) A father
   (C) An old alley cat
   (D) Ruth Stiles Gannett

2. Based on the information in the sentence below, how would you describe the alley cat **before** she met the narrator's father?
   This surprised the cat—she had never before met anyone who cared about old alley cats—but she said, "I'd be very much obliged if I could sit by a warm furnace, and perhaps have a saucer of milk." (Paragraph 2)
   (A) Bored
   (B) Tired
   (C) Lonely
   (D) Angry

3. What is the meaning of **obliged** as it is used in the following sentence? "I'd be very much **obliged** if I could sit by a warm furnace, and perhaps have a saucer of milk."
   (A) Annoyed
   (B) Thankful
   (C) Surprised
   (D) Proud

4. What does the cat say he will do for the little boy?
   (A) Be his friend forever.
   (B) Take him on an exciting journey.
   (C) Get him an airplane.
   (D) Find a way for him to fly while he's still young.

5. What sentence from the passage supports your answer to question 4?
   (A) My father said, "When I grow up I'm going to have an airplane. Wouldn't it be wonderful to fly just anywhere you might think of!" (Paragraph 4)
   (B) "Well," said the cat, "If you'd really like to fly that much, I think I know of a sort of a way you might get to fly while you're still a little boy." (Paragraph 7)
   (C) "My father and the cat became good friends." (Paragraph 3)
   (D) "You mean you know where I could get an airplane?" (Paragraph 8)

6. What is the meaning of the word **drippy** in the following sentence?
    One cold rainy day when my father was a little boy, he met an old alley cat on his street. The cat was very **drippy** and uncomfortable so my father said, "Wouldn't you like to come home with me?"

    (A) Cold

    (B) Sad

    (C) Dirty

    (D) Wet

7. How does the text's image contribute to the story?

    (A) It shows readers that the cat is cute.

    (B) It emphasizes that the cat was sad before meeting the boy.

    (C) It helps readers visualize the setting.

    (D) It makes the text more interesting.

8. What does Paragraph 3 add to the passage?

    (A) It tells readers more about the little boy.

    (B) It explains the story's conflict.

    (C) It helps readers understand the cat and the boy's relationship.

    (D) It builds suspense.

Directions: Read the passage "The Little Doll" and then answer Numbers 9 through 16.

Passage 2: The Little Doll
by Charles Kingsley

1   I once had a sweet little doll, dears,
     The prettiest doll in the world;
     Her cheeks were so red and so white; dears,
     And her hair was so charmingly curled.

2   But I lost my poor little doll, dears,
     As I played in the heath one day;
     And I cried for her more than a week, dears;
     But I never could find where she lay.

3   I found my poor little doll, dears,
     As I played in the heath one day:
     Folks say she is terrible changed, dears,
     For her paint is all washed away,
     And her arm trodden off by the cows, dears,
     And her hair not the least bit curled:
     Yet for old sakes' sake she is still, dears,
     The prettiest doll in the world.

9. What is the speaker's point of view in this poem?
      Ⓐ First person
      Ⓑ Second person
      Ⓒ Third person
      Ⓓ Third person limited

10. How many stanzas are in this poem?
      Ⓐ 16
      Ⓑ 3
      Ⓒ None
      Ⓓ 4

11. Complete the following sequence of events from the poem.
	(1) The child owns a beautiful doll.
	(2) ?
	(3) The child cries about the lost doll for more than a week.
	(4) The child finds the doll.
	(5) ?

	(A) (2) The child loses the doll; (5) The doll is ruined, and the child gives her away.
	(B) (2) Someone takes the child's doll; (5) The doll looks just the same as before.
	(C) (2) The child loses the doll; (5) The doll is changed, but the child still loves her.
	(D) (2) Someone takes the child's doll; (5) The child is upset that her doll has changed.

12. What is one way the doll does NOT change from the beginning of the poem to the end?
	(A) Her hair doesn't curl anymore.
	(B) Her paint comes off.
	(C) She loses an arm.
	(D) In the narrator's opinion, she is still the most beautiful doll in the world.

13. What does **heath** most likely mean in the following line from the poem?
	But I lost my poor little doll, dears
	As I played in the **heath** one day...
	(A) A beach
	(B) An area of open land
	(C) A type of candy bar
	(D) A lake

14. Which of the following is a life lesson that readers can learn from this poem?
- (A) Never play in the heath.
- (B) Appearance doesn't matter.
- (C) You can't trust everyone.
- (D) Don't take your toys outside.

15. Which line from the poem supports your answer to question 14?
- (A) "But I lost my poor little doll, dears, As I played in the heath one day..."
- (B) "Folks say she is terrible changed, dears, For her paint is all washed away..."
- (C) "And I cried for her more than a week, dears; But I never could find where she lay."
- (D) "Yet for old sakes' sake she is still, dears, The prettiest doll in the world."

16. What does the second stanza add to the story?
- (A) It introduces the main character.
- (B) It introduces the main character's problem.
- (C) It gives readers a description of the doll.
- (D) It helps readers learn more about the main character's personality.

Directions: Read the passage "Helping Nature to Help Us" and then answer Numbers 17 through 24.

Passage 3: Helping Nature to Help Us

1   By now, you've probably heard about global warming and climate change. These topics are a little complicated, but scientists know that our planet is getting hotter, and that's not good. Humans are the main cause of climate change.

How Do Humans Cause Climate Change?

2   Some gases in Earth's atmosphere trap heat and keep it from escaping. When heat can't escape, the Earth gets hotter. These gases are called "greenhouse gases," and they include carbon dioxide and methane.

3   People release more carbon dioxide into the atmosphere when they cut down trees, waste electricity, burn fuels like gas, and more. The more carbon dioxide we release into the environment, the more heat gets trapped on Earth, and the hotter it gets.

How Can I Reduce My Carbon Footprint?

4   Your carbon footprint is the amount of carbon dioxide that gets released because of you and your activities. If you want to help the environment, you can start by reducing your carbon footprint.

5   Turn off lights, the TV, and other electronics when you aren't using them. Encourage your family to walk or ride bikes instead of taking the car everywhere. Next time you go to a fast food restaurant, walk inside instead of sitting in the drive through with the car running.

Other Ways to Help the Planet

6   There are other things you can do to help our planet, too. Recycle, take shorter showers, and plant a tree or a fruit/vegetable garden. When you're older, you might want to choose a "green career." These are jobs that help take care of our planet and solve problems like climate change.

Now answer Numbers 18 through 24. Base your answers on the passage "Helping Nature to Help Us".

17. What is the main idea of the passage?
  (A) Humans are harming the planet, but there are steps we can take to help.
  (B) The planet is in danger, but there isn't much we can do about it.
  (C) Earth is getting hotter because of gases like carbon dioxide.
  (D) Everyone should try to reduce their carbon footprint.

18. What does **reducing** mean as it is used in this sentence from the passage?

If you want to help the environment, you can start by **reducing** your carbon footprint.

(A) Increasing, or making larger

(B) Getting rid of

(C) Decreasing, or making smaller

(D) Learning about

19. Which information can be found under the heading **How Do Humans Cause Climate Change?**

(A) The opinions of famous scientists

(B) Information about greenhouse gases

(C) Information about how people can stop causing climate change

(D) The definition of climate change

20. Based on the information in the passage, with which statement would the author most likely agree?

(A) Humans aren't to blame for climate change or global warming.

(B) If we want to save our planet, we should never ride in cars.

(C) People can take small steps, like planting a tree, to help the planet.

(D) There's nothing we can do to stop the planet from getting warmer.

21. Which piece of evidence from the passage supports your answer in question 20?

(A) "Your carbon footprint is the amount of carbon dioxide that gets released because of you and your activities." (Paragraph 4)

(B) "People release more carbon dioxide into the atmosphere when they cut down trees, waste electricity, burn fuels like gas, and more." (Paragraph 3)

(C) "By now, you've probably heard about global warming and climate change. These topics are a little complicated, but scientists know that our planet is getting hotter, and that's not good." (Paragraph 1)

(D) "There are other things you can do to help our planet, too. Recycle, take shorter showers, and plant a tree or a fruit/vegetable garden." (Paragraph 6)

23. How do greenhouse gases cause global warming?

(A) They trap heat, which causes the Earth to get hotter.

(B) They release more heat into the atmosphere.

(C) They pollute the planet.

(D) They kill trees and dry up oceans, which increases heat.

24. Which sentence in the passage supports your answer in question 23?

(A) "People release more carbon dioxide into the atmosphere when they cut down trees, waste electricity, burn fuels like gas, and more." (Paragraph 3)

(B) "Your carbon footprint is the amount of carbon dioxide that gets released because of you and your activities." (Paragraph 4)

(C) "The more carbon dioxide we release into the environment, the more heat gets trapped on Earth, and the hotter it gets." (Paragraph 3)

(D) "When you're older, you might want to choose a "green career." These are jobs that help take care of our planet and solve problems like climate change." (Paragraph 6)

ELA
Practice Test One

Session Two
(Writing)

Directions: Read the passage "The Fisherman and His Wife" and answer Numbers 25 through 26.

Passage 4: The Fisherman and His Wife

1   Once upon a time a fisherman who lived with his wife in a little, old shack close by the sea, and every day he went out fishing.

2   One day, he caught a flounder. The flounder said to him, "Please fisherman, let me live! I'm not really a flounder, but an enchanted prince."

3   The fisherman let the magic fish go, and then he went home to his wife in the little, old shack.

4   "Husband," said his wife, "Didn't you catch any fish today?"

5   "I did catch a flounder," said the man. "But he said he was really an enchanted prince, so I let him go."

6   "Didn't you wish for anything?" said his wife. "It's hard to always live in this disgusting, smelly, old shack.. Go back and call the fish. Tell him we want to have a new hut, he will surely give us that."

7   The man went back to the sea and called to the magic fish. "My wife says I should have made a wish," he told the fish. "She wants a new hut."

8   "Go home," said the flounder. "She has her wish already."

9   When the man went home, a new hut had replaced the dirty, old, shack. His wife showed him how much better the hut was, and they were very happy.

10   About two weeks later, the man's wife decided the hut was too small. This time, his wife wished for a great stone castle. The fish granted her wish again. But she still wasn't satisfied.

11   Next, the wife wished that she and her husband could be king and queen. The flounder obliged the wife again. She was happy, but not for long. No matter what wishes the flounder granted, the wife always wanted more.

12   Finally, she told her husband, "Just tell the fish to give me everything I deserve."

13   The man told the flounder about his wife's wish, and the flounder said, "Go home, her wish has already been granted."

14   When the man returned home, he found his wife crying. The stone castle had been transformed back into a little, old shack.

Now answer Numbers 25 through 26. Base your answers on the passage "The Fisherman and His Wife".

25. Write a summary of what happened in this story.

_____

_____

_____

_____

_____

_____

_____

_____

_____

_____

_____

_____

_____

_____

_____

26. What life lesson can readers learn from this story? Use evidence from the text to support your answer.

_____

_____

_____

_____

_____

Directions: Read the passages "Hummingbird" and "Honey Badgers" then answer Numbers 27 through 31.

Passage 5: Hummingbirds

1   If you've ever been close to a hummingbird, you've probably heard the buzzing noise they make when they fly. Hummingbirds make this noise because of how quickly they can flap their wings. They can beat their wings as many as 80 times in a single second! This gives them the ability to hover in the air, like a helicopter. Hummingbirds are also the only bird that flies backwards.

2   Moving so fast requires a lot of energy. This means that hummingbirds need to eat more than you would expect for such a small bird. Their favorite food is nectar, a sweet liquid that can be found inside flowers. Hummingbirds have to visit hundreds of flowers to get enough nectar each day. Every day, they drink more than their body weight in nectar.

3   It looks like hummingbirds use their long beaks like straws, but they really use their tongues to drink nectar. They lap up nectar from flowers the same way your dog or cat might lap up water from a bowl.

4   Flowers feed hummingbirds and help them gain energy, but hummingbirds help flowers too. When hummingbirds drink nectar, they get pollen from the flowers on their heads and beaks. Pollen is what helps flowers make seeds.

5   As the hummingbirds fly to more flowers to drink more nectar, they also spread pollen and help flowers make more seeds. Then more flowers grow, and the hummingbird has even more nectar to drink!

Now answer Numbers 27 through 28. Base your answers on the passages "Hummingbird."

27. According to the passage **"Hummingbird"**, why do hummingbirds require so much energy? Use a detail from the passage to support your answer.

_____

_____

28. How would you describe the relationship between hummingbirds and flowers? Use a
    detail from the passage to support your answer.

Passage 6: Honey Badgers

1   Honey badgers aren't very big, but they sure are tough. They're only a couple feet long and weigh just over 20 pounds, but they've been known to chase away lions. After they chase away the lions, they take the food the lions have hunted and eat it for themselves instead.

2   How can such a tiny animal be so tough? The honey badger is equipped with helpful weapons. For example, honey badgers have extremely thick skin. Arrows, bites from other animals, and even small bullets can't pierce the honey badgers' tough skin. Honey badger's teeth are strong too. A honey badger can bite through a turtle shell.

3   Honey badgers also have long, sharp claws. The claws are great for fighting off predators, but they're also useful for digging. Honey badgers can dig a nine-foot tunnel in just 10 minutes. They use this ability to construct their homes, which are small tunnels in the ground. If any predator approaches the honey badger's home, even a cow or a horse, the honey badgers will attack fiercely to defend their territory.

4   If honey badgers are so ferocious, why do they have such a "sweet" name? Well, honey badgers love to eat honey. Because their skin is so tough, they can invade beehives without being injured with bee stings. Beekeepers in Africa have to use electric fences to keep honey badgers from eating all of the honey their bees produce.

Now answer Numbers 29 through 31. Base your answers on the passages "Hummingbird" and "Honey Badgers".

29. What is the main idea of the passage **"Honey Badgers"**? Use **at least two** details from the passage to support your answer.

_____

_____

30. What do the illustrations in both the **"Hummingbird"** and **"Honey Badgers"** passages add to these passages?

31. You will now write your own article on the hummingbird and honey badger.

Based on the information in the passages, describe a similarity or a difference between the two creatures. Explain your answer using details from **both** passages.

Then, decide whether you think the hummingbird or the honey badger is more helpful to their habitat and environment. Which one do you think is more helfpul? Explain your answer using details from **both** passages.

The two passges are:
"Hummingbird"
"Honey Badgers"

_____

_____

_____

_____

_____

_____

_____

_____

_____

_____

_____

_____

_____

_____

ELA
Practice Test Two

Session One
(Reading)

Directions: Read the passage "Ancient Egyptian Pyramids" then answer Numbers 1 through 6.

Passage 1: Ancient Egyptian Pyramids

1   Many Ancient Egyptian pyramids are still standing today, and they're some of the most magnificent structures ever built by humans.

Why Were the Pyramids Built?

2   The pyramids were built as monuments and burial places to honor the pharaohs. Ancient Egyptians believed the pharaohs needed certain items in the afterlife, so the pharaohs were buried with all kinds of treasure. Some pharaohs were even buried with gold and silver boats for their "journey" to the afterlife.

Types of Pyramids

3   Not all pyramids look the same. Many early pyramids have large ledges that look like steps, so they're called "step pyramids." Experts think the Ancient Egyptians believed that the steps would help the pharaohs climb up to the sun god.

4   Pyramids built later have flat, sloping sides. The Ancient Egyptians believed that the sun god created the other gods and goddesses while standing on a mound. These later pyramids are designed to represent the mound.

How Were the Pyramids Built?

5   It's still a mystery exactly how the pyramids were built. The Ancient Egyptians had no modern machinery to build these giant structures.

6   Experts think thousands of people were required to cut up the large blocks, then slowly move them up the pyramid using ramps. Because the pyramids were built block by block, the building process was long and tedious.

7   Scientists estimate that it took 23 years and at least 20,000 workers to build the Great Pyramid of Giza. Most pharaohs ordered work on their pyramids to begin as soon as they became pharaoh, knowing that the process would take years.

Now answer Numbers 1 through 6. Base your answers on the passage "Ancient Egyptian Pyramids".

1. What is the main idea of the passage "Ancient Egyptian Pyramids"?
   (A) Pyramids are some of the most impressive man-made structures.
   (B) There are different types of pyramids.
   (C) The Ancient Egyptian pyramids were used to honor the pharaohs.
   (D) Scientists aren't completely sure how the pyramids were built.

2. Which information can be found under the heading "Why Were the Pyramids Built"?
   (A) The size of the pyramids
   (B) Ancient Egyptian beliefs about the afterlife
   (C) The number of people it took to build the pyramids
   (D) Ancient Egyptian beliefs about the sun god

3. What does the word mound mean as it is used in the following sentences?
   The Ancient Egyptians believed that the sun god created the other gods and goddesses while standing on a mound. These later pyramids are designed to represent the mound.
   (A) A staircase
   (B) A ladder
   (C) A tower
   (D) A hill

4. Based on the information in the passage, with which statement would the author most likely agree?
   (A) The pyramids took too long to build.
   (B) The pharaohs were selfish to have their treasure buried with them in the pyramids.
   (C) The Ancient Egyptian pyramids are very impressive structures.
   (D) Buildings built with modern machinery are better than the pyramids.

5. Which of the following did Ancient Egyptians believe about the afterlife?

    (A) You can take items with you to the afterlife.

    (B) There is no afterlife.

    (C) There's no way to prepare for the afterlife.

    (D) You can't take any earthly possessions with you to the afterlife.

6. Why did the author include Paragraph 7?

    (A) To introduce a problem.

    (B) To show that the pharaohs were selfish and impatient.

    (C) To emphasize the time and effort it took to build the pyramids.

    (D) To solve the mystery of how pyramids were built.

Directions: Read the passage "The Story of Fidgety Philip," then answer Numbers 7 through 12.

Passage 2: The Story of Fidgety Philip
by Heinrich Hoffman

1   "Let me see if Philip can
Be a little gentleman;
Let me see if he is able
To sit still for once at table":
Thus Papa bade Phil behave;
And Mamma looked very grave.
But fidgety Phil,
He won't sit still;
He wriggles,
And giggles,
And then, I declare,
Swings backwards and forwards,
And tilts up his chair,
Just like any rocking horse--
"Philip! I am getting cross!"

2   See the naughty, restless child
Growing still more rude and wild,
Till his chair falls over quite.
Philip screams with all his might,
Catches at the cloth, but then
That makes matters worse again.
Down upon the ground they fall,
Glasses, plates, knives, forks, and all.
How Mamma did fret and frown,
When she saw them tumbling down!
And Papa made such a face!
Philip is in sad disgrace.

3   Where is Philip, where is he?
Fairly covered up you see!
Cloth and all are lying on him;
He has pulled down all upon him.
What a terrible to-do!
Dishes, glasses, snapt in two!
Here a knife, and there a fork!

Philip, this is cruel work.
Table all so bare, and ah!
Poor Papa, and poor Mamma
Look quite cross, and wonder how
They shall have their dinner now.

Now answer Numbers 7 through 12. Base your answers on the passage "The Story of Fidgety Philip".

7. Based on the information in the poem, what does the word fidgety mean?
   Ⓐ Naughty
   Ⓑ Unable to sit still
   Ⓒ Funny
   Ⓓ Smart

8. How many stanzas are in this poem?
   Ⓐ 3
   Ⓑ 39
   Ⓒ None
   Ⓓ 4

9. Why are Papa and Mamma wondering how they can have their dinner now?
   Ⓐ The food is cold.
   Ⓑ Philip was naughty and ate all the food.
   Ⓒ Philip pulled down the tablecloth, silverware, plates, and food.
   Ⓓ Dinner still isn't ready.

10. Select the missing item from this sequence.
   (1) Papa asks Philip to see if he can sit still for once.
   (2) Philip won't sit still, and he starts to tilt his chair back.
   (3) ?
   (4) Philip grabs the tablecloth and pulls everything down on top of him.

   Ⓐ Philip gets in trouble and is asked to leave the table.
   Ⓑ Philip's mother tells him to stop tilting the chair back.
   Ⓒ Philip's chair starts to fall, and Philip screams.
   Ⓓ Philip says he's not hungry.

11. What does the second stanza add to the poem?
   Ⓐ It shows the consequences of Philip's actions.

(B) It gives us more information about the main character.

(C) It helps readers understand the setting.

(D) It introduces the conflict.

12. How does Philip's behavior change from the beginning of the poem to the end of the poem?

(A) It doesn't change.

(B) Philip stops fidgeting in his seat.

(C) Philip listens to his parents and stops being naughty.

(D) Philip won't listen to his parents at first, but he apologizes after pulling down the tablecloth.

Directions: Read the passage "The Pony Express" then answer Numbers 13 through 18.

Passage 3: The Pony Express

1   Today, we can communicate with people across the country with a quick text or phone call. In the 1860's, it wasn't so easy.

Communication in the 1860's

2   When the United States was first settled, the settlers lived in the eastern part of the United States. But in the 1840's, pioneers started moving west. In 1848, thousands of settlers headed west because gold had been discovered in California, and people were hoping to profit.

3   Of course, this made it difficult for people to communicate with their family on the other side of the country. There was no phone, the train line to California wasn't yet completed, and it could take months to travel across the country by horse.

The Pony Express System

4   So how did people communicate? They used the Pony Express. It would take most people weeks, months, or even a year to travel across the country. The Pony Express could deliver messages along this same trail in just 10 days.

5   How was this possible? The Pony Express had 184 stations set up from the West to the East. Each station was ten miles apart, and ten miles is about the distance a horse can gallop without getting tired. At each station, the rider would get a new horse.

6   The riders were allowed to rest too. Each rider had home stations every 75-100 miles along the trail. At the home station, the rider was permitted to rest. While he rested, the rider would hand his mail to another Pony Express rider. This way, the mail never stopped moving, even while the horses and riders got some rest.

Pony Express Riders

7   Most of the Pony Express riders were teenage boys. This was because Pony Express riders had to be light and travel fast. The riders were required to weigh under 125 pounds.

8   The riders also had to be in great shape. On the average day, they rode at least 100 miles at a fast pace. In an emergency, they might be expected to ride 200 miles in a single day. The ride was often dangerous, and riders were sometimes attacked by Native Americans or by wild animals.

9   Despite the dangers and difficulties, Pony Express riders lost only one mail pouch the entire time the Pony Express was running.

The End of the Pony Express

10 However, the Pony Express didn't run for long. It only lasted from 1860-1861. The Civil War started in April of 1861. In October, the first telegraph line to California was completed. With telegraphs, people could send messages instantly.

11 Two days after the telegraph line was finished, the Pony Express closed for good. But the strength and bravery of its riders remain legendary today.

Now answer Numbers 13 through 18. Base your answers on the passage "The Pony Express".

13. How did the building of the telegraph line affect the Pony Express?
    Ⓐ The riders didn't have to deliver as much mail, since there was now another way to communicate.
    Ⓑ The telegraph line didn't have a major effect on the Pony Express.
    Ⓒ The telegraph line caused the Pony Express to close, since people could now send messages instantly.
    Ⓓ The telegraph line made people appreciate the Pony Express even more.

14. Which information can be found under the heading "Pony Express Riders"?
    Ⓐ Why the Pony Express was needed
    Ⓑ How the Pony Express managed to deliver mail so quickly
    Ⓒ What caused the Pony Express to close
    Ⓓ How far Pony Express messengers traveled in a single day

15. With which statement would the author of this passage most likely agree?
    Ⓐ Although the Pony Express didn't run for long, it's an impressive and interesting part of history.
    Ⓑ The Pony Express delivered mail too slowly.
    Ⓒ The Pony Express was too dangerous for its riders.
    Ⓓ The Pony Express isn't important because it was quickly replaced with faster ways to communicate.
    (Paragraph 10)

16. What is the main idea of this passage?

    (A) The Pony Express rides were difficult and dangerous, but they only lost one mail pouch.

    (B) The Pony Express took only 10 days to travel a trail that took most people weeks or months.

    (C) Communication used to be difficult, and the Pony Express was one legendary solution to this problem.

    (D) The Pony Express only lasted from 1860-1861 before being replaced by the telegraph.

17. What does profit mean as used in this sentence from the passage?
In 1848, thousands of settlers headed west because gold had been discovered in California, and people were hoping to profit.

    (A) Discover something

    (B) Enjoy something

    (C) Make money

    (D) Benefit from something

18. Why were most of the Pony Express riders teenage boys?

    (A) Older men weren't interested in riding for the Pony Express.

    (B) The pay was low, so only teenagers were willing to do the job.

    (C) Teenagers liked the risk and danger, why older people were afraid of it.

    (D) The riders had to be light and fast.

Directions: Read the passage "The Ugly Duckling" then answer Numbers 19 through 24.

Passage 4: Excerpt from The Ugly Duckling
by Hans Christian Andersen

1   It was lovely summer weather. In a sunny spot stood a pleasant old farm-house, and from the house down to the water side grew great burdock leaves, so high, that under the tallest of them a little child could stand upright. In this snug retreat sat a duck on her nest, watching for her young brood to hatch. At length one shell cracked, and then another. From each egg came a living creature that lifted its head and cried, "Peep, peep."

2   "Quack, quack," said the mother, and then they all quacked as well as they could. "Are you all out?" she continued, rising; "No, I declare, the largest egg lies there still. I wonder how long this is to last, I am quite tired of it;" and she seated herself again on the nest.

3   "Well, how are you getting on?" asked an old duck, who paid her a visit.

4   "One egg is not hatched yet," said the duck, "it will not break. But just look at all the others, are they not the prettiest little ducklings you ever saw?"

5   "Let me see the egg that will not break," said the duck; "I have no doubt it is a turkey's egg. I was persuaded to hatch some once, and after all my care and trouble with the young ones, they were afraid of the water. I quacked and clucked, but all to no purpose. I could not get them to venture in. Let me look at the egg. Yes, that is a turkey's egg; take my advice, leave it where it is and teach the other children to swim."

6   "I think I will sit on it a little while longer," said the duck; "as I have sat so long already, a few days will be nothing."

7   "Please yourself," said the old duck, and she went away.

8   At last the large egg broke, and a young one crept forth crying, "Peep, peep." It was very large and ugly. The duck stared at it and exclaimed, "It is very large and not at all like the others. I wonder if it really is a turkey. We shall soon find it out, however when we go to the water. It must go in, if I have to push it myself."

9   On the next day the weather was delightful, and the sun shone brightly on the green burdock leaves, so the mother duck took her young brood down to the water, and jumped in with a splash. The water closed over their heads, but they came up again in an instant, and swam about quite prettily with their legs paddling under them as easily as possible, and the ugly duckling was also in the water swimming with them.

10   "Oh," said the mother, "that is not a turkey; how well he uses his legs, and how

upright he holds himself! He is my own child, and he is not so very ugly after all if you look at him properly. Quack, quack! come with me now, I will take you into grand society, and introduce you to the farmyard, but you must keep close to me or you may be trodden upon; and, above all, beware of the cat."

Now answer Numbers 19 through 24. Base your answers on the passage "Excerpt from The Ugly Duckling".

19. What is the meaning of **snug** as it is used in the following sentence from the text?
It was lovely summer weather. In a sunny spot stood a pleasant old farm-house, and from the house down to the water side grew great burdock leaves, so high, that under the tallest of them a little child could stand upright. In this **snug** retreat sat a duck on her nest...
  - (A) Cozy
  - (B) Uncomfortable
  - (C) Old
  - (D) Large

20. What convinces the mother duck that the "ugly duckling" really is her own child and not a turkey?
  - (A) When he hatches and says, "Peep, peep!"
  - (B) When she realizes he looks just like her
  - (C) When he's able to swim well like the other ducklings
  - (D) When he calls her "Mommy"

21. Who is the narrator of this story?
  - (A) The mother duck
  - (B) The ugly duckling
  - (C) The old duck
  - (D) A third person narrator who's not part of the story

22. Based on the information in the passage, how can you describe the mother duck?
  - (A) She's mean to her children.
  - (B) She cares about what other animals think.
  - (C) She doesn't like the ugly duckling.
  - (D) She's a good mother who loves her children.

23. Why does the mother duck start to think the ugly duckling might be a turkey?
  - (A) He looks like a turkey.
  - (B) He is larger and doesn't look like the other ducklings.
  - (C) He can't swim like the other ducklings.
  - (D) He sounds like a turkey instead of a duck.

24. Based on the information in the story, how does the mother duck feel about sitting on the eggs?

(A) She enjoys it.

(B) She thinks it's boring and would rather do something else.

(C) She thinks it's uncomfortable.

(D) She's getting tired of sitting on the eggs for so long.

ELA
Practice Test Two

Session Two
(Writing)

Directions: Read the passage "The Evolution of the Telephone" then answer Numbers 25 through 26.

Passage 5: The Evolution of the Telephone

1 Today, we have pocket-sized cell phones that can be used as calculators, cameras, calendars, mini computers, flashlights, and much more. Even thirty years ago, this would have seemed impossible.

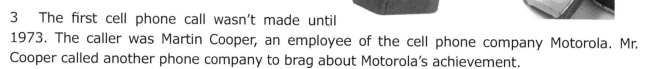

2 The first transmission of the human voice was in 1876. The inventor of the telephone, Alexander Graham Bell, spoke to his assistant over the phone, saying, "Mr. Watson, come here. I want to see you." By 1956, telephones were being used to call people in other countries.

3 The first cell phone call wasn't made until 1973. The caller was Martin Cooper, an employee of the cell phone company Motorola. Mr. Cooper called another phone company to brag about Motorola's achievement.

4 Ten years later, Motorola started selling cell phones to the public. The first cell phone cost $3,995 and weighed almost two pounds. It took ten hours to charge the cell phone.

5 In Motorola's commercial, they predicted that one day, the sight of people checking their cell phones would be as common as the sight of people checking their watches.

6 Cell phones got smaller, cheaper, and more popular in the 1990's. In 1992, the first text message was sent. It said, "Merry Christmas." In 2000, the first camera phone was released in stores in Japan.

7 Smart phones were introduced in 2007 with Apple's first iPhone. Android was introduced by Google soon after, in 2008. Since then, even more improvements have been made to the smartphone. And it turns out Motorola's prediction was correct: 95% of American adults currently own a cell phone.

Now answer Numbers 25 through 26. Base your answers on the passage "The Evolution of the Telephone".

25. How have cell phones changed since the first cell phone was released? Use evidence from the text to support your answer.

_____

_____

_____

_____

_____

_____

_____

_____

_____

26. What information does the picture help readers understand? Use evidence from the text to support your answer.

_____

_____

_____

_____

_____

_____

_____

_____

_____

Directions: Read the passage "The Country Mouse and the City Mouse" and answer Numbers 27 through 28.

Passage 6: The Country Mouse and the City Mouse

1   Once a little mouse who lived in the country invited a little Mouse from the city to visit him. When the little City Mouse sat down to dinner he was surprised to find that the Country Mouse had nothing to eat except barley and grain.

2   "Really," he said, "you do not live well at all; you should see how I live! I have all sorts of fine things to eat every day. You must come to visit me and see how nice it is to live in the city."

3   The little Country Mouse was glad to do this, and after a while he went to the city to visit his friend.

4   The very first place that the City Mouse took the Country Mouse to see was the kitchen cupboard of the house where he lived. There, on the lowest shelf, behind some stone jars, stood a big paper bag of brown sugar. The little City Mouse gnawed a hole in the bag and invited his friend to nibble for himself.

5   The two little mice nibbled and nibbled, and the Country Mouse thought he had never tasted anything so delicious in his life. He was just thinking how lucky the City Mouse was, when suddenly the door opened with a bang, and in came the cook to get some flour.

6   "Run!" whispered the City Mouse. And they ran as fast as they could to the little hole where they had come in. The little Country Mouse was shaking all over when they got safely away, but the little City Mouse said, "That is nothing; she will soon go away and then we can go back."

7   "This is very terrible," said the little Country Mouse; "let us not go back to the cupboard again."

8   "No," said the City Mouse, "I will take you to the cellar; there is something special there."

9   So the City Mouse took his little friend down the cellar stairs and into a big cupboard where there were many shelves. On the shelves were jars of butter, and cheeses in bags and out of bags. Overhead hung bunches of sausages, and there were spicy apples in barrels standing about. It smelled so good that it went to the little Country Mouse's head. He ran along the shelf and nibbled at a cheese here, and a bit of butter there, until he saw an especially rich, very delicious-smelling piece of cheese on a queer little stand in a corner. He was just on the point of putting his teeth into the cheese when the City Mouse saw him.

10   "Stop! stop!" cried the City Mouse. "That is a trap!"

11   The little Country Mouse stopped and said, "What is a trap?"

12   "That thing is a trap," said the little City Mouse. "The minute you touch the cheese with your teeth something comes down on your head hard, and you won't survive."

13 The little Country Mouse looked at the trap, and he looked at the cheese, and he looked at the little City Mouse. "If you'll excuse me," he said, "I think I will go home. I'd rather have barley and grain to eat and eat it in peace and comfort, than have brown sugar and dried prunes and cheese,—and be frightened to death all the time!"

14 So the little Country Mouse went back to his home, and there he stayed all the rest of his life.

Now answer Numbers 27 through 28. Base your answers on the passage "The Country Mouse and the City Mouse"

27. Does the **country mouse** like the city or country better? Use evidence from the passage **"The Country Mouse and the City Mouse"** to support your answer.

_____

_____

_____

_____

_____

_____

_____

28. Does the **city mouse** have a different point of view on **the city** than the country mouse? Use evidence from the passage **"The Country Mouse and the City Mouse"** to support your answer.

_____

_____

_____

_____

_____

_____

Now answer Numbers 29 through 30. Base your answers on the passage "The Boy Who Cried Wolf".

Passage 7: The Boy Who Cried Wolf

1   There was once a shepherd-boy who kept his flock at a little distance from the village. Once he thought he would play a trick on the villagers and have some fun at their expense. So he ran toward the village crying out, with all his might,—

2   "Wolf! Wolf! Come and help! The wolves are at my lambs!"

3   The kind villagers left their work and ran to the field to help him. But when they got there the boy laughed at them for their pains; there was no wolf there.

4   Still another day the boy tried the same trick, and the villagers came running to help and got laughed at again. Then one day a wolf did break into the fold and began attacking the lambs. In great fright, the boy ran for help. "Wolf! Wolf!" he screamed. "There is a wolf in the flock! Help!"

5   The villagers heard him, but they thought it was another mean trick; no one paid the least attention, or went near him. And the shepherd-boy lost all his sheep.

29. Describe the changes in the characters' attitudes (both the villagers and the boy) from the beginning of the passage **"The Boy Who Cried Wolf"**? to the end. Use details from the passage to support your answer.

_____

_____

_____

_____

_____

_____

_____

_____

_____

30. Would the author of the passage **"The Boy Who Cried Wolf"** agree with the following statement: **"**Honesty is always the best choice". Use details from the passage to support your answer.

_____

_____

_____

_____

_____

_____

_____

_____

_____

_____

_____

31. Your teacher has asked you write about a life lesson you learned from each of the passages **"The Country Mouse and the City Mouse"** and **"The Boy Who Cried Wolf"** Use evidence from **both** passages to support your answer. Are the lessons you learned similar or different?

Practice Tests
One & Two
Answer Key & Explanations

ELA PRACTICE TEST ONE
Answer Explanations
Session 1 (Reading)

1. **A.** The narrator of this story is a son or daughter. Although the story focuses on the father, it his son or daughter who is telling readers about something that happened to the father as a young boy. **(RL.2.6)**

2. **C.** The cat seems lonely based on the provided information. The cat is surprised by the boy's kindness because "she had never before met anyone who cared about old alley cats." Readers can infer that if the cat has never met anyone who cared about her, then she has been very lonely. **(RL.1.3)**

3. **B.** The cat would be thankful to have something to drink and a warm place to rest, especially because no one has showed her kindness in the past. **(RL.2.4)**

4. **D.** The cat says he might know a way for the child to fly while he's still a little boy.

5. **B.** This quote indicates that the cat will help the boy fly while he's still young. The rest of the text makes it clear that while she will help the boy fly, it won't be with an airplane. **(RL.1.1)**

6. **D.** Wet. The passage explains that it is raining when the boy finds the cat, so we can infer that "drippy" is referring to the cat being wet, with rain dripping from its fur. **(RL.2.4)**

7. **B.** The image emphasizes that the cat was sad prior to meeting the boy. It helps readers visualize how the cat looked when the boy ran into him and understand why the boy felt compelled to treat the cat so kindly. **(RL.3.7)**

8. **C.** Paragraph 3 gives readers information about the cat and the boy's relationship, explaining that they have developed a close friendship. **(RL.2.5)**

9. **A.** This poem is written in first person. We know this based on the speaker's use of words such as "I" and "my." **(RL.2.6)**

10. **B.** This poem contains three stanzas. **(RL.2.5)**

11. **C.** After readers are introduced to the child and the beautiful doll, the child loses the doll. When the doll is eventually found, she has changed physically: Her hair doesn't curl anymore, she's missing an arm, etc. However, the child still loves her and finds her to be the most beautiful doll in the world. **(RL.1.2)**

12. **D.** All of the physical changes listed in A-C do happen to the doll, but the narrator's opinion of the doll does not change as a result. To the narrator, the doll is still the prettiest in the world. **(RL.1.1, RL.1.3)**

13. **B.** An area of open land. This is the only answer choice that makes sense in the context of the poem. A lake wouldn't make sense because the child would probably have never found the doll, and the doll would have been wet if she was found. A beach wouldn't make sense because the doll would have probably been covered in sand and water if she was found. **(RL.2.4)**

14. **B.** The best answer is, "Appearance doesn't matter." The poem teaches this lesson as the child continues to love her doll and view her as "the prettiest doll in the world" despite the fact that she is now missing paint, an arm, and her charming curls. Answer Choice D is a lesson that could be learned, but not the main lesson of this poem.

15. **D.** This quote supports answer 14 because the speaker mentions that her doll is "still" the prettiest in the world. The speaker explains that this is because of "old sakes' sake," indicating that the speaker's feelings for the doll and memories with the doll matter more than the doll's appearance.

16. **B.** The second stanza introduces the main character's problem (the doll is lost, and the main

character is devastated). **(RL.2.5)**

17. **A.** This answer adequately summarizes the main idea of the passage. Choice B is untrue, and choices C and D only cover specific parts of the passage, rather than the main idea of the passage as a whole. The passage is about the damage humans are doing to the planet, in addition to the steps we can take to help. **(RI.1.2)**

18. **C.** Students can help the planet by making their carbon footprint smaller. Students should infer that they can't get rid of their carbon footprint altogether, because they will sometimes use electricity, drive or ride in cars, etc. **(RI.2.4)**

19. **B.** Information about greenhouse gases can be found under the heading "How Do Humans Cause Climate Change?" To answer the questions, students must be able to locate the appropriate heading and skim the information presented. **(RI.2.5)**

20. **C.** The author would agree with the statement that people can take small steps, like planting a tree, to help the planet. Other statements are too extreme, like we should "never" ride in cars or there's nothing people can do to help the planet.

21. **D.** This quote from the passage shows the author's belief that there are things people can do to help the planet, such as planting trees. **(RI.2.6)**

23. **A.** Greenhouse gases trap heat. When heat can't escape, the planet gets hotter.

24. **C.** This quote directly explains how greenhouse gases heat Earth and cause global warming. **(RI.1.1)**

ELA Practice Test One
Session 2 (Writing)

25. The man catches a flounder. He lets go of the fish which is actually an enchanted prince. The man's wife tells him to go back to the fish and wish for a new hut instead of an old shack, and the fish grants the wish. The wife asks for a stone castle, and the fish grants the wish. The wife wishes to be king and queen, and the wish is granted. The wife then wishes for everything she deserves, and the castle is transformed into a little, old shack again.

26. This story teaches the lesson that we should be grateful for what we have. No matter what the magic fish gave to the wife, she was never happy and always wanted more. At the end of the story, the wife asked the fish to give her everything she deserves, so he gave her the old shack again. Because the wife couldn't be grateful and appreciate what she had,

the fish thought she deserved nothing more. One piece of evidence that supports this answer is the quote "No matter what wishes the flounder granted, the wife always wanted more." (Paragraph 11) as it shows that the wife was ungrateful and couldn't be satisfied. **(RL.1.1, RL.1.2)**

27. Hummingbirds need energy because they move so quickly. The passage explains that although hummingbirds are small, they must eat a lot to help them maintain the energy to beat their wings so quickly. Hummingbirds beat their wings as many as 80 times in a single second. **(RI.1.1)**

28. Hummingbirds and flowers have a helpful relationship. The flowers feed and provide energy to the hummingbirds, and the hummingbirds help pollinate the flowers. **(RI.1.3)**

29. Answers will vary. A main idea of this passage is that honey badgers are much tougher than they look. The passage starts off by mentioning that honey badgers are relatively small, but the rest of the passage focuses on all the ways honey badgers are more tough and ferocious than one would expect. Some details to support this point include that honey badgers, although small, use their strong teeth, sharp claws, and tough skin to protect themselves and fight predators. Also, even though a honey badger is only a couple feet long and weigh just over 20 pounds, they've been known to chase away lions. The quote about the badgers defending their homes against even horses and cows, who are much bigger than the honey badger, also supports the main idea. **(RI.1.2)**

30. The illustrations help readers see and understand the information in the passages about hummingbirds and honey badgers. For example, readers can see the small size of both the honey badger (compared to the tuft of grass) and hummingbird (compared to flower). They can see the honey badger's sharp claws and the hummingbird's hovering. **(RI.3.7)**

31. Answers will vary. One similarity is that both the creatures are small in size but can do things that you would not expect as they are small. For example, hummingbirds eat much more food than one would expect, and honey badgers are far more fierce than one would think. **(RI.3.9)** The hummingbird is more helpful to its environment. It pollinates flowers and helps them grow. Nothing in the passage suggests that the honey badger does anything helpful. It explains that he takes food from lions, defends himself and his home ferociously, and steals honey from bees.

(RI.3.9, RI.1.1)

ELA PRACTICE TEST TWO
Answer Explanations
Session 1 (Reading)

1. **A.** The main idea of the passage is that pyramids are some of the most impressive man-made structures. The passage goes on to provide more information about pyramids and why they are so magnificent. **(RI.1.2)**

2. **B.** Under the heading "Why Were the Pyramids Built", the author explains that the pyramids were built as burial sites and monuments to honor the pharaohs. The section also goes into more detail about how the pharaohs were buried, including the fact that treasure was "sent with them" to the afterlife. The sun god isn't mentioned until the heading "Types of Pyramids."**(RI.2.5)**

3. **D.** A mound is a hill. Students can determine this information based on the context provided, in addition to the picture of the "mound" pyramid. The pyramid in the 2nd image does not resemble a staircase, ladder, or tower. **(RI.2.4)**

4. **C.** The author would agree that the pyramids are impressive. There's nothing in the passage to suggest that the author thinks the pyramids took too long to build, that the pharaohs were selfish, or that buildings built with modern machinery are superior. **(RI.1.1, RI.2.6)**

5. **A.** The Ancient Egyptians believed you could take items with you to the afterlife, as demonstrated by details about the pharaohs being buried with treasure and even boats for the journey. The quote about pharaoh's "needing certain items for the afterlife" and being buried with treasure shows that the Egyptians believed you could take items with you that you would need in the afterlife. **(RI.1.1)**

6. **C.** Paragraph 7 emphasizes the time and effort that it took to build the pyramids, using a specific example. **(RI.3.8)**

7. **B.** Fidgety means unable to sit still. At the beginning of the poem, Philip's father tells him to try sitting still for once, but Philip is unable to do so. He eventually starts rocking his chair back and forth, causing the chair to fall. Philip desperately makes a grab at the tablecloth, but he ends up just pulling the tablecloth down on top of himself, all because he is fidgety. **(RL.2.4)**

8. **A.** This poem contains three stanzas. **(RL.2.5)**

9. **C.** Papa and Mamma can't eat dinner because Philip has pulled down the tablecloth, along with the contents of the table: dishes, food, plates, cups, silverware, etc. **(RL.1.1, RL.2.5)**

10. **C.** Philip's chair starts to fall, and Philip screams. This is what causes Philip to grab the tablecloth, resulting in a ruined dinner. **(RL.1.2)**

11. **A.** The second stanza shows the consequences of Philip's actions. He has been disobeying his parents and fidgeting, but in the second stanza he screams as his chair begins to fall. He ends up pulling down the tablecloth and the contents of his table on top of himself. The conflict is further developed in this stanza, but it is first introduced at the very start of the poem. **(RL.2.5)**

12. **A.** Philip's behavior does not change over the course of the poem. He fidgets from beginning to end. It's possible that his behavior may change now that he has experienced consequences, but there's no evidence to suggest this. **(RL.1.3)**

13. **C.** The telegraph line allowed people to send messages instantly, instead of the ten days required to deliver mail through the Pony Express. Two days after the telegraph line opened, the Pony Express closed. **(RI.1.3)**

14. **D.** Under this heading, readers can find information about how far the riders had to travel each day. The section explains that most of the riders were light, fast teenagers who were in shape enough to travel at least 100 miles per day. **(RI.2.5)**

15. **A.** The author seems to have a positive view of the Pony Express, and choice A is the only answer that shows a favorable opinion of the Pony Express. **(RI.2.6, RI.1.1)**

16. **C.** This is the only choice that covers the overall idea of the passage. The other options are too specific, covering only small pieces of the passage. This passage is about the fact that communication was previously far more complicated than it is today, and the Pony Express was one interesting and impressive way that this problem was solved. **(RI.1.2)**

17. **C.** Profit means to make money. People traveled to the West in hopes of striking it rich with the California Gold Rush. The gold had already been discovered, and they didn't only want to enjoy or benefit from the gold. Specifically, people hoped to make money. **(RI.2.4)**

18. **D.** The riders had to be light and fast, so most of them were teenagers who weighed under 125 pounds. **(RI.1.1)**

19. **A.** Snug means cozy. The tone of the paragraph, with words like "lovely," "sunny," and "pleasant," makes it clear that the mother's retreat is pleasant and comfortable. **(RL.2.4)**

20. **C.** The mother realizes the duckling is not a

turkey when he's able to swim with his siblings. Previously, she said that the duckling might be a turkey, but she would know for sure once she took him swimming. The old duck had told the mother duck that when she hatched turkeys, they weren't able to swim and didn't even want to go in the water. **(RL.1.1, RL.1.3)**

21. **D.** The narrator is a third person narrator who is not part of the story. We know this because the narrator never uses the word "I" or "we." **(RL.2.6)**

22. **D.** The mother duck is a good mother who loves her children. When the old duck tells her to stop sitting on the large egg, the mother duck refuses and says she would be willing to sit for a few more days. She talks about how beautiful her ducklings are, and once she realizes that the ugly duckling is indeed her child, she also comments that he isn't so ugly after all. **(RL.1.3, RL.1.1)**

23. **B.** Mother duck begins to think that the ugly duckling might be a turkey after he hatches. She says that it is very large, ugly, and doesn't look like the other ducklings. **(RL.1.1)**

24. **D.** The mother duck is getting tired of sitting on the eggs for so long. She questions when the large egg will finally hatch because she is tiring of sitting on the eggs. The text does not specify that she is uncomfortable or bored, and she doesn't seem to enjoy it. **(RL.1.3)**

ELA Practice Test Two
Session 2 (Writing)

25. Answers may vary slightly. Cell phones have gotten smaller, cheaper, and more popular. This information is provided in the text in Paragraph 6. The first cell phone cost $3,995 and weighed almost two pounds. 95% of adult Americans now own cell phones. Students may also mention that cell phones charge much more quickly now. The first cell phone took ten hours to charge. Cell phones can send text messages now (the first text was sent in 1992) and can take pictures (the first camera phone was released in 2000). **(RI.1.3, RI.1.1)**

26. The picture helps readers understand what the first cell phone looked like and how different it is from the modern cell phone. The text mentions that the cell phone weighed almost two pounds, but it's easier for readers to visualize how big the phone was when looking at the images. One of the images also places the first cell phone side by side with a modern phone, which emphasizes the way cell phones have changed over the years. **(RI.3.7)**

27. Answers will vary. The country mouse likes the country better. Even though he like some of the food in the city like brown sugar and dried prunes and

cheese, he did not like that people chase mice and set traps for mice. He likes the peace and comfort of the country where he does not have to worry about being killed. At the end of the story, he says he would rather have barley and grain to eat than be frightened to death all the time. **(RL.1.1)**

28. Answers will vary. The city mouse has a different point of view than the country mouse about the city. He knows a lot about the city, but is not frightened of all the things that happen in the city. For example, the country mouse doesn't notice the traps that could kill him, but the city mouse knows about the danger of the trap. He shouts at the country mouse to be careful. This shows that they both have different points of views about the city. **(RL.2.6)**

29. Answers will vary. At first, the villagers are caring. In the story, they're described as kind and willing to help the boy. Later, they no longer trust the boy and refuse to help him. The boy starts off being naughty. He tricks and frightens the villagers about a wolf. Later, he learns that lying was not a good idea because the villagers won't help him when he really needs them. **(RL.1.3)**

30. Answers will vary. An appropriate student response could be: The author would agree with this statement because the story shows that when the boy did not tell the truth, bad things happened to him, such as his sheep being eaten by the wolves. At first, the villagers are caring and willing to help the boy. However after he is dishonest several times, they decide not to help him. In the end, the villagers ignore him because they don't trust him and they think he is dishonest. The author shows that being dishonest can lead to a bad situation. **(RL.2.6)**

31. Answers will vary. The first passage teaches readers to be grateful for what they have, but the second focuses more on the dangers of lying. In the first passage, the mouse learns to be happy with what he has. His country life may not be filled with fine foods, but he's able to be safe, comfortable, and at peace. The quote near the end of the story supports this answer: the mouse has learned that brown sugar and cheese aren't worth more than peace, safety, and comfort. In the second passage, it is shown that you shouldn't lie, because you'll lose people's trust. The villagers trusted the boy and tried to help him the first two times, but they realized they had been tricked. When there really was a wolf, the villagers didn't trust the boy enough to believe him, and the boy lost all of his sheep. The life lessons are different from each other in this example. **(RL.3.9, RL.2.6, RL.1.2)**

Made in the USA
Columbia, SC
06 November 2021

48463663R00080